Increase Niles Tarbox

Songs and Hymns for Common Life

Increase Niles Tarbox

Songs and Hymns for Common Life

ISBN/EAN: 9783744652285

Printed in Europe, USA, Canada, Australia, Japan

Cover: Foto ©Thomas Meinert / pixelio.de

More available books at **www.hansebooks.com**

SONGS AND HYMNS

FOR

COMMON LIFE.

BY
INCREASE N. TARBOX.

BOSTON:
PRINTED FOR THE AUTHOR,
BY DAVID CLAPP & SON.
1885.

Affectionately Inscribed

TO MY DAUGHTERS,

SUSIE WATERS CARR AND MARY PORTER RAYMOND,

IN MEMORY OF

THEIR BELOVED MOTHER,

THE poems contained in this volume have been written in the intervals of a somewhat busy life. They are published now, not for the general market, but for distribution among friends. Many of them have appeared, from time to time, during the last thirty-five years, in the columns of the *Boston Congregationalist*. A few have been published in other periodicals; while a considerable number of them are put in type now for the first time.

I. N. T.

INDEX

Ancient Sabbath School	128
Absalom	185
Anglo-Saxon Whittling Song	193
Battle of the Wilderness	44
Bunker Hill	63
Bewildered Prophet	90
Black Valley Railroad	106
.Baptismal Hymn	127
Boston-ology	223
Banishment of Cupid	247
Boston Yankee Doodle	249
Cæsar and Christ	42
Christian Old Age	101
Christmas Carols	143 and 144
Centennial Celebration at Tolland, Conn.	158
Church of Old Windsor, Conn., 1630–1880	173
Change of the Moon	212

Crinoline 251
China and America 252
December 21st, 1620–1870 . . . 78
Dedication of School House . . . 120
Dedication of Hitchcock Library Hall . 129
Dedication of a City Hall 221
Death in our Home 257
Evening 30
Earth's Wonders 47
Evening at Cape Ann 57
Easter Hymns 138–142
First Thanksgiving, 1621 97
First Psalm 115
Forefathers' Day 116
God 1
Great Pan is dead 21
Great City at Midnight . . . 53
God in the Garden 146
Golden Weddings . . . 197–207
Game of Courtesy 248
House by the Sea 49
Heaven is far and Earth is near . . . 93
Hymn for Peace 117
Hymns for Freedom . . . 154 and 155
I dwell among mine own people . . 67

Installation at Old South,—Hymn	135
Jerusalem	28
Jubilate Deo	157
Job IV. 12–17	136
Jackson Falls, N. H., and Old Dog Spring	210
Kings	39
Matter or Spirit	8
Mountain Spring	34
Midnight Train	70
Mystery of the Stars	100
My Little Playmate	111
My Mother's Grave	240
Northeaster	5
Nellie	37
New Settlements	145
Nocturn	156
Old Meeting-House	82
Omniscience	122
Our Native Land	123
Our Land	126
Our Fathers	133
Open Fire	244
Plymouth and the Bay	82
Pilgrim Father, Reconstructed	84
Psalm VIII.	134

INDEX.

Pride of Ancestry	230
Rest of Waking	19
Ripe for Heaven	77
Revolutionary Tea	214
Saintly Women	59
Snow Storm	68
Song for May Day	113
Safety of the State	118
Sabbath School Celebration	121
Song for Freedom	132
Song of the Redeemed	137
Still Small Voice	152
Silver Wedding	207
Socrates and the Hemlock	232
Summer Rest	255
Toil and Rest	51
Two Songs	54
"Tell About"	91
They that Watch for the Morning	94
The Unknown Land	96
Thanksgiving	103
Time for Thanksgiving	109
The Good Man's Death	119
Torn Battle Flags	153
The Old Chestnut Tree	219

The River of God	237
"Thou Bethlehem"	243
To Whom it may Concern	253
Visions of the Night	25
Vanished Faces	72
Who saw the Star	55
Winter Night	61
When I first went down to Yale	187
Yale Songs	147–151
Yale College	227
Zion's Glory	124

SONGS AND HYMNS.

GOD.

This Being, great and high;
This Name majestic sounding o'er the earth:
Who thought this thought, gave this conception birth,
    Beneath the vaulted sky?

Who dreamed this wondrous dream,
Of ONE, that binds all worlds about his throne,
And claims dominion for Himself alone,
    Farther than light can gleam,—

Hiding in realms of air,
Making the unknown heavens his shining home,
Or down th' abyss, deeper than thought can roam,
    Dwelling in mystery there,—

So holy, good and just,
That the unfallen angels, great in might,
Veil their pure faces at the dazzling sight,
    And bow them to the dust,—

Who gave this thought its birth?
Who by his searching found out such a God,
And sent the marvellous story far abroad,
    Over our fallen earth?

———

The deep and sounding sea,
Rolling forever on its restless track,
From its mysterious caverns thunders back—
    This thought came not from me.

No bird, on sweeping wing,
Has traced its source in all her airy round:
No vulture's eye the hidden place has found,
    Or known its secret spring.

Old empires in their might,
With kings in proud succession on their thrones,
Bowed down in awe to senseless stocks and stones,
    In one long pagan night.

Egypt, with all her lore,
Lifting her ponderous pillars to the sky,
Bent to the ox in low stupidity,
    Worshipped,—and knew no more.

Beneath the eastern sun,
Where Tigris hastes to join her sister stream,
Assyria sat and dreamed her mighty dream,
    Till her full race was run;

But not, in all her thought,
Did God, the Unseen Ruler, find a place;
Nebo and Bel, and all that hideous race,
    Were the poor gods she sought.

Tyre, with her white-winged fleets,
Nestled in beauty by the Central sea,
Where snowy Hermon, rising grand and free,
    Looked on her busy streets,—

Worshipped the Queen of Night,
The foul Astarté, with her rites profane,
Or bowed beneath old Moloch's bloody reign,
    And fed his grim delight.

And Greece, the young and fair,
Brightest of nations; with her keen-eyed thought,
In all her subtle dreamings, vainly sought
    This highest thought to share;

Wondering and overawed,
Searching for something which she could not find,
Builded her altar, with bewildered mind,
    To one—the Unknown God.

This Being, great and high;
This Name majestic sounding o'er the earth,
Who thought this thought, gave this conception birth,
    Beneath the vaulted sky?

"In Judah God was known:"
While yet the earth lay wrapt in pagan night,
O'er these rough hills and round fair Salem's height,
    A heavenly glory shone.

"In Zion was His place:"
With Israel's marshalled hosts His name was great:
He sat a Monarch, throned in holy state,
    Amid his chosen race.

"Lift up your heads, ye gates"!
The God, whose power the highest heaven fills,
Comes to His temple, built on Zion's hills;
"The King of glory waits"!

"Lift up your heads, ye gates!
"And be ye lift, ye everlasting doors"!
The Monarch comes to tread your hallowed floors,
"The King of Glory waits"!

"Who is this King of Glory"?
And heaven answers, with its tides of song,
"The Lord of Hosts—the Lord in battle strong,
"He is the King of Glory."

On through the circling years,
While ancient empires hasted to decay,
And the broad lands in pagan darkness lay,
Wrapt in their gloomy fears,—

This light on Zion shone:
It sparkled in her glancing mountain rills,
It bathed in splendor Judah's rugged hills,
And rested there alone,—

Till the set time was come:
Till angels sang our Great Messiah's birth:
Then this great Name went forth to fill the earth
And make the world its home.

Whence did this thought arise?
Guide us, ye sophists, to its unknown source;
Lead us along to trace its hidden course,
Ye knowing ones and wise.

This Being, great and high;
This Name majestic sounding through the earth;
Who thought this thought, gave this conception birth,
Beneath the vaulted sky?

THE NORTH-EASTER.

"Then comes with an awful roar,
   Gathering and sounding on,
The storm-wind from Labrador,
The wind Euroclydon,
     The storm-wind."—LONGFELLOW.

EVEN now the heralds tell it,
   The gloomy omens say,
This mighty storm-wind, from afar,
   Is on its sounding way.
There is moaning through the forest;
   The restless clouds hang low;
They scud along the mountain sides,
   Surcharged with wind and snow.

House well the shivering cattle,
   And fold the bleating sheep,
And guard the yawning crevices,
   Where icy currents creep:
Heap high the blazing hearth-stone,
   And close the shutters tight,
The tempest, in its furious march,
   Will break on us to-night.

THE NORTH-EASTER.

Now gather round the fireside,
    And watch its dreamy glow;
And hark!—upon the window pane
    The rustle of the snow!
Mid the fast gathering darkness,
    Hear the strange, mournful wail,
The wild song which the tempest sings,
    The anthem of the gale.

O'er high and shaggy mountains,
    By village, field and dell;
Around the scattered cottages
    Where lonely toilers dwell;
Far, far away, this wailing song
    Through all the land is heard;
And many a fancy wakes to-night,
    And many a heart is stirred.

We see, enwrapt in vision,
    The grand and awful form
Of ONE, who in the darkness hides,
    And rides upon the storm:
And now He moves in majesty;
    His chariot is the cloud,
And at the tumult of his march,
    The stoutest heart is bowed.

But oh! the toiling mariner,
    Tossed helpless on the deep;
Drifting where mountain billows break
    Along the rocky steep.

THE NORTH-EASTER.

In vain his sad, despairing cry,
    In this tumultuous hour,
The sea is roaring for its prey,
    And ready to devour.

Some mother watches by the fire,
    In cottage, far away,
And dreaming of her sailor boy,
    Hums the old cradle lay:
Ah, well for her!—she cannot hear
    This far-resounding roar,
Nor see the wild work going on
    Along the savage shore.

God help the lonely wanderer!
    Bewildered in the storm;
Struggling along his blinded path
    With bowed and shivering form:
Lost in the howling darkness,
    How can his heart be bold?
For who can fight the winds of night,
    Or stand against the cold?

We sit and think of one who sleeps
    In her sweet wood-land grave,
And hears no more the angry roar
    Where earth-born tempests rave:
But human hearts are poor and weak,
    And feel a chilling dread,
At the wild uproar of the storm
    Around her lonely bed.

Open the door-way softly,
  And look out on the world:
See the mad tempest sweeping by,
  Its mighty wings unfurled:
Then bless the bounteous Giver
  For the fireside's genial glow;
For the roof that gives thee shelter
  From storm and cold and snow.

This wind that raves so madly,
  Howling with fiendish will,
Has yet the artist's gentle touch,
  The sculptor's cunning skill:
And when the morn comes breaking,
  O'er all the world shall stand
Pure forms of chiselled beauty,
  Wrought by her magic hand.

MATTER OR SPIRIT.

They tell me that our modern lore,
Sounding through nature to the core,
Transcends all wisdom known before:

That ancient myth and faith are dead;
That henceforth, it shall rest unread
What the old bards and prophets said.

They tell me, they alone are wise,
Who walk by their own searching eyes,
And put no trust in mysteries:

Who follow what the mind can know,
In these material fields below,
And let the unseen wonders go:

Who ply the chemist's subtle trade,
And think, by its most potent aid,
To tell how first the worlds were made;

Or, skirting the primeval morn,
How, from the ancient night forlorn,
Out of dead matter, life was born.

———

I urge the cravings of the soul,
Which mounts above this earthly pole,
And ranges in the boundless whole;

Which rising heavenward, leaps and sings,
Soaring on swift ethereal wings,
Beyond these low and earth-born things;

Which moves in glory with the stars,
Far from the tumult and the jars
Of Earth, and her perplexing wars.

With such persuasions as I can,
I urge that in the general plan
Nature is nothing without Man:

These earthly fields, so large and fair;
The orbs, that move in upper air;
The bodies, which our Spirits wear;

Are all to higher ends designed,
And their great meaning only find,
As handmaids of the deathless Mind.

These arching heavens and rolling earth,
Cut loose from souls, of godlike birth,
With all their pomp, are nothing worth.

Why talk of souls?—they make reply,
Who knows of souls that never die,
But pass immortal to the sky?

What is the soul?—a subtle strain
Of music, issuing from the brain,
A joyous or a sad refrain;

This harp kind nature's touch may wake,
But who that task will undertake,
When once its trembling strings shall break?

The *body*, with its wondrous whole,
Wheel within wheel, in mystic roll,
Emits that wonder called *the soul*.

Nay, give this sweeping logic, pause;
How dost thou study Nature's laws?
Can the effect control the cause?

The floating fragrance, which the flower
Emits in summer's sunny hour,
Does it react with kingly power?

Can music, when its notes are rung,
And once on wandering breezes flung,
Control the harp from which it sprung?

Borne on soft wings, the mellow strain
Dies out amid the wind and rain;
It goes, but comes not back again.

So, if the soul its being draws
From earthly and organic laws,
Still flowing outward from its cause,

As light comes streaming from the sun,
Or brooklets from the mountains run;
How are its works of wonder done?

The soul sits sovereign on a throne:
It has an empire all its own,
Where, by its will, it rules alone.

In busy day, and silent night,
It grapples, with a giant's might,
The august problems of the right.

The soul may sing with angel choirs,
Even while the quivering frame expires,
Enwrapt in raging martyr-fires.

It bends the body to its will,
Bids the wild rebel lusts, be still;
Bids the whole man its tasks fulfil.

It sets itself what task it please,
To weigh the stars, or sound the seas,
And the poor brain minds its decrees.

Is this the efflux of a brain,
Dropping like falling drops of rain,
Or as the wheat-stalk sheds the grain?

But the old voice comes back to me:
Tell, if thou hast the power to see,
How in the acorn dwells the tree?

Around thy pathway, every day,
Ten thousand organisms play,
Each in its own mysterious way.

Unfold that strange and subtle power,
Which works in silence, hour by hour,
To weave the splendor of the flower.

How are those golden fruits begun,
Which, when the summer days are done,
Hang mellow in the autumn sun?

Or can thy daring thought aspire,
To track that darting throb of fire,
Which leaps along the electric wire?

Then by what wisdom art thou taught,
When sense, and nerve, and brain have wrought,
To prove the product is not *thought?*

MATTER OR SPIRIT.

Nay, nay, this logic does not suit:
We nourish Nature, at the root,
And wait, in patience, for the fruit.

We set our chosen tree with care,
To catch the sun, the rain, the air,
And bide what fruitage it shall bear.

So now, to make your logic plain,
Go feed your child with milk and grain,
And wait the efflux of the brain.

Leave what you call the soul, alone:
'Tis a resultant, all unknown,
Until the wonder shall be grown.

Keep the young nursling well apart
From books and every learnèd art,
And see what thoughts from flesh will start.

Go now, all free and unconfined,
And by this food of earthly kind,
Build us a Newton's towering mind.

You dare not follow by your rule;
You put the unseen soul to school,
Or let the child grow up a fool.

Since earth was born, or time began,
None ever acted on the plan
That the frail body was the man.

Sages, from age to age, have wrought
Upon an unseen soul, and sought
How best to wake its latent thought.

For wrapt in slumbering infancy,
All ready to take wings and fly
Its wondrous intuitions lie.

Thoughts which no sense could e'er impart,
And strange emotions of the heart
Out of this hidden world shall start.

Its subtle food wastes not away,
But while all earthly stores decay
Its garners grow from day to day.

All treasured wisdom of the past,
All that the ages have amassed,
Becomes its heritage at last.

But if you wish—call man a brute:
Pray tell us now what wondrous fruit
Will spring and grow from such a root?

Suppose you victor in this chase:
For you and me, how stands the case?
And what good cometh to the race?

You tell us that you seek for light,
That day is better than the night,
That safety always dwells with right.

MATTER OR SPIRIT.

You search for truth, what way you can,
For truth, in nature's boundless plan,
Will work the glory of the man.

Fair words—but words for shame and tears,
If life, with all its hopes and fears,
Ends with these transitory years.

Yea what is truth?—go ask the flocks,
That sleep amid the hillside rocks:
Go ask the dull contented ox;

Truth is for them, as well as you,
If, when the earthly life is through,
Dark night forever shuts the view.

O prate not with these hollow sounds;
Your words are only jingling rounds,
If man leaps not these mortal bounds.

There is no truth—there is no right:
And night is day, and day is night,
If from beyond there comes no light.

Yea, bind my conscience, if you can,
Upon this low material plan;
What law or rule am I to scan?

If I do right—I meet the curse;
If I do wrong, 'tis hardly worse;
The payman holds an empty purse.

MATTER OR SPIRIT.

Come let us eat, while blood runs high,
And drink, as the swift moments fly,
For on the morrow we shall die.

Yea, let us haste to seize our prey,
In the dark night, when best we may,
And hide us in our dens by day.

And from the conscience, let us clear
That idle rubbish of a fear
Lest some great judgment-day be near.

Why should we walk beneath that dread,
While the fierce lion makes his bed
In peace—if only he be fed?

———

O man! abate this foolish pride:
Look up, the starry heavens are wide,
And mystery dwells on every side.

Small reach has all thy boasted lore:
If false—how poor and mean the store!
If true—still meaner than before!

Why walk abroad in pomp and show?
We see how far your search can go;
We know how little you can know.

That ancient Book, which you despise,
Grows doubly precious in our eyes,
The more these low-browed systems rise.

'Tis a dark corner where you dwell,
Like some old hermit in his cell,
With head bowed down, his beads to tell.

'Tis a broad universe of light
The Bible opens to our sight,
Where winds are free, and stars are bright.

We boast in what that record saith,
That Man is God's immortal breath,
Born for the years that know no death.

We joy in David's lofty page,
Still sounding on from age to age,
Though kings combine, and heathen rage;

In rapt Isaiah's piercing ken,
Which saw the coming ages, when
God's kingdom should come down to men.

And our poor sinning, suffering race,
Still has in God its hiding-place,
And wears a glory on its face.

Leave the poor pilgrim, when he dies,
The sweet hope that his soul shall rise
To join the armies of the skies;

That when the dust returns to dust,
The mortal shall give back its trust,
To go and dwell among the just;

That friends, long parted, shall await
His coming at the heavenly gate,
And set him with the good and great.

In these rough pathways, while we plod,
Let us believe the Son of God
Along these earthly ways has trod;

That He from highest heaven came down,
With love, unchecked by earthly frown,
Our manhood with his own to crown.

Let us believe that Jesus died
To take away our sin and pride,
And set us with the sanctified;

That on the morning of that day,
When the great stone was rolled away,
The grave was thwarted of its prey;

That from the mountain's holy height,
He vanished from our mortal sight,
And hid himself in heaven's own light.

Call this delusion, if you will;
It fills a place, earth cannot fill,
And sheds o'er man a glory still.

Rise from the dust and walk abroad;
Bow down, with wonder over-awed,
And ask for wisdom from your God.

THE REST OF WAKING.

I WANDERED helpless in the land of sleep,
   In a wild tangled wilderness of dreaming,
Where toiling hard some beaten path to keep,
   All hope went out in vague and fitful gleaming;
It was a dark, strange, phantom land of fear,
   A land whose sights and sounds were full of sorrow,
Each wandering voice was hateful to the ear,
   And no fixed guiding light the soul could borrow.

All toil was nought—in vain each laboring groan,
   In vain all art and skill and bold endeavor,
Condemned like Sisyphus to roll the stone,
   Which slipped the grasp, and still rolled back forever:
As some poor hare, caught in the hunter's net,
   Frenzied with fear, now struggling, now despairing,
Finds with each strain the coil more firmly set,—
   Such was the sum of all my toilsome daring.

And demons foul, in every hideous form,
   Thronged round me, half in twilight shadows hiding,
Creatures, that find their pastime in the storm,
   Like sea-birds on the gloomy tempest riding.
But such wild slumber must, perforce, have end;
   Upon this dark a dawn must needs come breaking;
Some swelling horror proves the sleeper's friend,
   By sharp excess of agony awaking.

THE REST OF WAKING.

What blissful rest to waken from such sleep,
  From this long war of strange chaotic dreaming,
And find a midnight stillness calm and deep,
  And the soft moonlight through the casement streaming;
To hear no discord moving on the air;
  The full-orbed moon in peaceful splendor riding;
To see the stars shine down on landscapes fair,
  And know that God's strong hand the world is guiding!

O night so calm, so beautiful and still!
  O skies so deep and blue where stars are twinkling!
No voice or sound is heard, save from yon hill
  The pebbly brook sends out its silvery tinkling.
Luxurious rest!—to sit and dream and gaze,
  And slake the spirit at this fount of healing;
The earth enrobed in moonlight's magic haze,
  That dreamy veil, half-hiding, half-revealing.

And when death's sleep has sealed our weary eyes,
  And on the vision Heaven's glad morn is breaking,
When all the unknown wonders of the skies
  Burst on the soul from earth-born dreams awaking,
Will fairer worlds in holier beauty drest,
  Will softer landscapes on the sight come beaming,
Than this calm scene of stillness and of rest,
  To one who wakes from wild tumultuous dreaming?

GREAT PAN IS DEAD.

I.

In dim and shadowy ages long gone by,
　This sad and moaning cry
Went o'er the sunny Grecian lands:
By hill and dell and ocean sands,
　Through many a flowery vale,
　Echoed the lowly wail;
The mountain winds took up the tearful tale;
The shepherds ran, the mournful news to tell,
And maidens left their pitchers at the well:
　On, on the message sped,
　Great Pan is dead!

II.

　This was Arcadia's rural god:
And in her mountain cots, the faith was sweet,
　That Pan along her rocky pathways trod,
And made her whispering woods his fond retreat.
　It pleased the shepherd fancy day by day,
　That Pan looked on to see the young lambs play;
　To watch the white flocks on the grassy glade,
　Or safely sleeping in the noontide shade:
　　To him the shepherds piped their songs,
　　Told him their loves, and griefs, and wrongs;
　　And blushing maidens, without fear,
Whispered their hopes and sorrows in his ear:
　And now the glory of the earth has fled,
　Great Pan is dead!

III.

These were but simple children of the sun,
  Living their roving life among the hills,
Watching the stars their nightly circuits run,
  Tracking the wild paths of the mountain rills:
Little they knew of all that lay behind
  Those rocky heights that girded in their land;
How little of that One Eternal Mind
  Who holds the earth and stars in his right hand.
Pan was to them the wonder of the skies;
  He wove the robes of beauty round the earth;
Of him they talked with shining, happy eyes,
  Their god of festive joy and song and mirth:
And now they sit bowed down in grief and dread,
  Great Pan is dead!

IV.

  Great Pan is dead!
In low and mournful converse still they said,
And the whole earth sounds hollow to our tread:
  How can the silly lambkins play?
How can the birds pour forth their morning lay,
To usher in another weary day?
  Our oaten reeds are laid aside,
  The fields have lost their flowery pride,
And all is loneliness, since Pan has died.
  We sleep and wake, we wake and sleep,
  What is the fruit of all our toil?
Slowly the years around us creep,
  And death stands waiting for his spoil:
Our days are filled with fear and care and strife,
There is no charm to sweeten human life:

Our dull and dismal rounds we tread;
But the bright heavens have lost their ancient light;
O'er all the earth falls down a withering blight;
 Great Pan is dead!

V.

The rolling centuries move across the stage,
And we are children of a later age.
 The same sun gives us light,
The same stars sparkle in the heavenly height,
The same fair moon makes beautiful our night;
 The olden thoughts are still at play:
We walk beneath the same mysterious skies,
And know that death is watching for his prey,
 While we gaze onward with inquiring eyes:
 We have no might or power
Against the forces that around us roll;
God is our strength—our everlasting tower,
 The only refuge for the weary soul.

VI.

 But hark!—a strange, strange voice,
Sounding abroad from Learning's ancient halls,
An atheist voice—which boldly to us calls,
 There is no God—and let the earth rejoice:
The old beliefs have had their little day,
And now let wisdom hold her cheerful sway.
 Lend your inquiring glance:
Come see the star-dust in its mystic dance;
See the great planets form and wheel, by chance.
 The only god that guides their course,
 And speeds them on their burning way,
 Is that impersonated *force*,

Which asks no worship—will not hear you pray.
    Search the primeval morn;
    See how all life from death was born;
    And how, through woe and pain,
    All life goes back to death again.
What! do you sit with sad and drooping head?
That Hebrew God whom you have feared, is dead.
There is no God—so doff your robes of sadness,
And let your days resound with joy and gladness.

VII.

    Vainly these hollow accents fall;
The great, round world stops not to heed this call:
      Whatever sea we sound,
      Whatever land be trod,
In all the earth, no atheist race is found;
    Humanity's full heart cries out for God.
We shall not lose those rapt and lofty songs,   [young,
    Which bards and prophets sang when time was
Their inmost thought to the whole earth belongs,
    And their high strains shall never be unsung.
      By Conscience and her haunting fears;
      By Faith's great hope of after bliss,
      By all the inner spirit hears
      Of the eternal fitnesses,
    We shall not take these painted shells,
    In which no living creature dwells.
These mocking sounds upon the ear may roll,
But cannot cheat the longings of the soul.
    The glory fades along the starry sky;
      The beauty dies from earthly landscape fair;
    No splendor lights the unseen realms on high
      Except an Ever-Living God be there.

VISIONS OF THE NIGHT.

"In thoughts from the visions of the night, when deep sleep falleth on men."

In the still realm of dreams,
Folded in sleep, beneath the midnight shades,
The Past—as all the weary Present fades—
    Rises in fitful gleams.

The far off years are back:
Departed forms, long gone from mortal sight,
Fresh with their olden life, and sparkling light,
    Glide in on unseen track.

The mists are rolled away:
With open vision, face to face we stand:
We hear the voices,—grasp the friendly hand
    Of some long-vanished day.

Strange mystery of the mind!
These whisperings of sleep, unknown, unsought,
Bring back hid treasures, which the waking thought
    Searches in vain to find.

When in the glare of day,
We strain our gaze to reach those distant years,
How dim with shadows all the scene appears!
    How soon it melts away!

But dreams revive the dead:
No longer do they come to us from far;
No change has passed—we see them as they are,
    Life, light upon their head.

The maiden, whom we loved,
Comes forth to meet us at her father's door,
Waking the blissful thoughts, with which, of yore,
    Our inmost souls were moved.

The old emotions burn,
Beneath the ashes of extinguished fires;
Love's tender, pure and passionate desires
    Flame from their buried urn.

The wan and weary years,
When we went sorrowing for the loved and lost;
The long and waking nights, when anguish-tost,
    We wet our couch with tears;

These are but things of air:
Our life is fresh as in its dewy prime;
We heed no change,—we know no lapse of time;
    We banish every care.

The darling whom we left,
With bleeding hearts, in her low, silent bed,
Among the small and great—the countless dead—
    These many years has slept.

The seasons come and go:
Around her grave the flowers of summer bloom,
And the wild storms of winter wrap her tomb,
    In their white robes of snow.

But now she comes once more:
We hear her joyous prattle in the hall;
We join her frolic, answer back her call,
    Through the half-open door.

Her sunny ringlets wave,
As she goes bounding in her wild delight;
Our hearts go out rejoicing at the sight;
    We know no death, no grave.

When age has dimmed the eye;
When earth no more makes music in our ears,
These golden visions of departed years
    In dreams go flashing by.

If Sleep, with noiseless hand,
Can open thus the barred and rusted gates;
    If the forgotten Past obedient waits
        And comes at her command;

If, from their silent halls,
These slumbering memories, wakened by her spell,
Bursting the shadowy confines where they dwell,
    Come flocking when she calls;

Oh Death! what may not be,
When earth and sense are but forgotten things:
When, at thy touch, we rise on angel wings,
    And are forever free?

JERUSALEM.

Thy queenly name, Jerusalem!
    Goes journeying down the years,
Still wearing on its front a crown
    Of glory and of tears:
The songs that sounded on thy hills,
    When Adam's race was young,
Those lofty hymns to Israel's God
    Shall never be unsung.

Around thy walls old empires prowled,
    Like hungry beasts of prey;
Or hovering on thy mountain paths,
    In cunning ambush lay:
From age to age thy captive sons
    Went forth in weeping bands,
To toil beneath the bloody rod,
    In lonely tyrant lands.

Those empires now are ground to dust;
    While thine undying race
Still finds in God—its father's God—
    Some secret hiding-place:
The seed of Abraham is not lost;
    That tribe, of wondrous birth,
Still wanders as a scattered host
    In all the lands of earth.

Thy Temple, O Jerusalem!
    On Zion's lordly height,
Has shed on nations, near and far,
    A strange and holy light:
The watchman on thy towers beheld
    The glad unnumbered throngs—
The gathering tribes—that filled thy courts
    With their great festal songs.

From year to year, from age to age,
    The long processions flowed
Through all thy vales, and o'er thy hills,
    To Zion's blest abode;
Their white tents glistened on the slopes,
    While they, with one accord,
Told the old legends o'er, and sung
    High praises to the Lord.

Along thy streets, Jerusalem!
    The Man of Sorrows trod;
And thou did'st nail upon the cross
    The loving Son of God:
That record of thy sin and shame
    Was washed in thine own blood,
When War and Storm swept o'er thy walls,
    A wild devouring flood.

But over all thy shame and guilt,
    Thy stubbornness and pride,
The works which thou hast wrought for God
    Shall evermore abide:

Thy name shall still go sounding on
    To every race and clime;
A glorious and immortal name,
    That feels no touch of time.

Jerusalem! thine ancient grace
    Has gone beyond the sky,
To image forth that city fair,
    The saintly home on high.
We read the prophet's burning words,
    And wait the mandate, when
The New Jerusalem shall come
    From heaven, down to men.

EVENING.

GENTLY the dew falls on the grass,
    The winds are hushed to rest,
And softly sinks the crescent moon
    Adown the quiet west.

I sit upon the summer hills,
    Far from the noisy throng,
And hear the modest night-bird sing
    Her low and plaintive song.

The little streamlets, bright and clear,
    Go singing on their way,
While countless insect voices weave
    Their never-ending lay.

EVENING.

O God, in such an hour as this,
    How yearns the soul to know
The mysteries of the heavens above
    And of the earth below!

An atom in the boundless whole,
    A speck upon the air,
I seem as one engulfed and lost,
    Without a Father's care.

My life I draw, I know not how,
    From the mysterious past;
Before me stretches all unknown
    A future strange and vast.

What part have I in this wide realm?
    What place have I to fill?
Or can the smallest issue hang
    Upon my wavering will?

Yet folded in these shades of night,
    My busy thoughts arise,
To range afar the fields of earth,
    And wander through the skies.

Is there a hand that reaches down
    From out this vast unknown?
Is there a love that beckons me
    To the eternal throne?

I ask the silent stars above,
    As men have asked of old,
No voice comes from them, as they look
    On mountains still and cold.

The entrance of Thy Word, O God!
    Alone can break this night,
And shed o'er all the way I go
    The clear and living light.

By faith, I take that blessed Word,
    And follow at its call;
The God who made the heavens and earth,
    Can see and know them all.

THE OLD MEETING-HOUSE.

On the height of a lonely hill
    Its rusty old form it uprears,
Standing in solitude, where it has stood
    Through the storms of a hundred years.

The simple dwellers around,
    Like the tribes of old, could say,
" Come, let us go *up* to the house of the Lord,
    Let us tread in His courts to-day."

It meets the first rays of the morn,
    While the valleys still sleep in the shade,
The glories of sunset play round its walls,
    And it shines as with sapphires inlaid.

In the dark and stormy nights,
    When the tempests sweep over the hill,
It creaks in the blast, and wild, wild songs
    Its desolate corridors fill.

THE OLD MEETING-HOUSE.

But it stands in its ancient strength,
   It can bear the hurricane's shock,
It was built to endure, and its pillars rest
   On the firm and primitive rock.

The traveller sees it afar,
   On his rough and winding way;
The husbandman sees it, resting from toil,
   In the heats of the summer day.

Around it the multitudes sleep,
   Who of old sought its altars in prayer,
A great congregation, they rest from their toils,
   Unmoved by earth's tumult and care.

On headstones dim and decayed,
   We spell out the names of the dead,
And over their dust returned to the dust,
   In reverent silence tread.

O, many the thoughts of the heart,
   As we stand by this temple of God,
And think of the worshippers, vanished and gone,
   Who up to its courts had trod!

They came in the joy of their souls,
   Or they came with their burdens to bear,
In the sunlight of youth, in the evening of age,
   In hope, or in grief and despair.

O, strong is the tie that entwines!
   And subtle the mystical chord
That binds human souls, with their sorrows and sins,
   To the altar and house of the Lord!

Then peace to the church on the hill!
Where its rusty old form it uprears,
Let it stand in its loneliness, where it has stood
Through the storms of a hundred years!

THE MOUNTAIN SPRING.

THERE are no pathways like those olden ranges,
    Where, in our youth, with careless feet we strayed;
There are no waters now, so clear and sparkling,
    As the old streams along whose shores we played;
And as the years come darkly gathering round us,
    And life's high noon descends to shadowy night,
Home of our childhood! how the picture rises,
    In dreams and waking visions, on the sight!

I see a land of stern and shaggy uplands,
    With running brooks, and valleys rich in green,
Broad hillside pastures, rough, but sweet and verdant,
    Where, wandering free, the grazing flocks are seen;
A mountain world—far from the noise of cities,
    Away from all the restless haunts of men;
With lonely heights, and strange primeval forests,
    Romantic gorge, and deep secluded glen.

How grandly through these vales and mountain passes,
    The storms of winter rolled along their path!
Through the long nights we heard the fitful dirges
    Of the wild tempest, moaning in its wrath;

But when the moon, in full autumnal glory,
    Shed down her dreamy light upon these hills,
How like enchanted silence, broken only
    By the soft cadence of the glancing rills!

In a deep recess of a wooded valley,
    Close to the mountain's broad and rugged base,
A covert thick with shadows—where the sunlight
    Struggled through leafy folds to find the place,
A little spring came gushing from the hillside,
    From the cool caverns of that rock-ribbed land,
Whose waters, clear as crystal, ever rippling,
    Played in their little bed of shining sand.

Through all the changes of the fitful seasons,
    In summer's heat and in the winter's snow,
In drought and deluge, still the little fountain
    Sent out its waters in unchanging flow;
The mighty hills were its eternal balance,
    Its everlasting store-house of supply,
Still flowing on, while generations perish,
    And the old forest monarchs fail and die.

And gray-haired men repeat the tender story
    Of one who dwelt amid these mountain lands,
A man of flocks and herds and spreading acres,
    And wise in all the labor of his hands;
A man beloved and honored, tried and trusted,
    And in his happy home the joy and light,
Till o'er him fell a cloud of gloomy darkness,
    And all his day was changed to dismal night.

THE MOUNTAIN SPRING.

He dare not drink the pure refreshing water,
    Which from his own sweet mountain well he drew,
But he was minded of this hillside fountain,
    Where God sent forth his waters, ever new;
No evil hand could taint this limpid current,
    Fresh from the hidden chambers of the earth;
No arm of hate could reach the mystic channels,
    In which this crystal streamlet had its birth.

This was his rock of God, amid the desert,
    Where like a trusting child, he went to drink;
The way was long, the path was rough and toilsome,
    That led his footsteps to its shady brink;
But ever, as a burning thirst came o'er him,
    With weary feet he trod these forest ways,
And drank his fill, at this full-flowing fountain,
    And snatched brief memories of his better days.

The summer months passed slowly, and the autumn
    With all its leafy splendors glided by,
But, to his sight, the bright earth was a prison,
    And no autumnal glories cheered his eye;
But when the sharp winds of the early winter
    Swept through these valleys, with their icy breath,
His trembling limbs no more could bear their burden,
    And God sent down the sweet release of death.

Flow on, thou clear and pleasant hillside fountain!
    Though the years darken round my lonely way,
I know that others bend to drink thy waters,
    And happy children on thy borders play;

And while the world grows old, and nations vanish,
And the slow-rolling centuries come and go,
Like God's own love, unfailing and eternal,
Thy cooling current shall not cease to flow.

NELLIE.

The April morning on the hills
    Breaks peacefully and fair,
As if the earth was full of joy,
    And had no woes to bear:
The soft light falls on dewy fields,
    Fresh in their virgin green,
And swelling buds and opening leaves
    On every side are seen.

In at the open windows, pour
    The happy tides of song,
And all the air is resonant
    With music rich and strong;
How like a mockery in our ears,
    This chorus free and wild!
While we stand bending o'er our dead,
    Our dear and darling child.

But yesterday, when morning broke,
    Her song was full and free;
Her happy voice chimed in to meet
    This outward melody:

That happy voice is hushed and still,
    These hands their places keep;
These shining, starry eyes are closed
    In their eternal sleep.

'Tis all a dream—a strange, strange dream,
    What one short day has done:
The morning saw her in her joy,
    But at the setting sun
Her wandering mind and busy hands
    Filled all our hearts with dread,
And ere the evening hours had passed,
    She slept, as sleep the dead.

O God! how tender was thy love,
    When this dear child was given!
How precious was she in our sight,
    Fresh from her native heaven!
Her soul ran o'er with happiness
    From morning dawn till night,
And like some blessed angel guest
    She filled our home with light.

We bless Thee for the memories
    Of this dear loving child;
We bless Thee, that for four short years
    Upon our home she smiled:
For her pure, bright, unselfish life,
    Her winning words and ways;
And these sweet memories will we keep
    Through all our future days.

How beautiful in death she lies,
    In her cold, dreamless sleep:
O'er her fair head her sunny locks
    In careless ringlets creep:
Her lips, half-parted, bear a smile,
    As when she said *good night,*
And all her face seems sprinkled o'er
    With heaven's dawning light.

Go, loved one, to thy Father's house,
    To that pure home on high,
Where fresher fields and fairer flowers
    Shall open on thine eye:
To the dear Shepherd of the flock,
    Who waits with arms outspread,
That he may lay his gentle hands
    In blessings on thy head.

KINGS.

The mightiest kings the rolling years have known,
    Stretching their empire farthest o'er the earth,
Are men who knew no splendors of a throne,
    No place of princely birth.

They saw God's glory on the mountain heights;
    They traced His handiwork in starry skies;
All nature spread her wealth of fair delights
    Before their wondering eyes.

In the far shadows of the ancient days,
   Went forth a stranger from Chaldean lands,
Wandering from clime to clime through unknown ways,
   Still led by unseen hands.

The world lay dark before his pilgrim feet,
   As he toiled onward, lonely and unblest,
Seeking through winter storm and summer heat
   To find his land of rest.

Yet from this wanderer sprang that wondrous race,
   Which lived while ancient empires went and came,
And now the patriarch holds on earth a place
   Beyond all kingly fame.

Along the banks where Nilus rolls his tide,
   Sleeps the proud dust of Egypt's early kings;
While the low wind, from the far desert side,
   Its mournful requiem sings.

These haughty tyrants, stained with shame and guilt,
   Thought to defy the wasting touch of time,
By giant tombs, which toiling thousands built
   Beneath that burning clime.

Lo, now! These sepulchres in mockery stand;
   Their chambers empty as an echoing shell;
Of those old kings—all that they thought and planned
   They have no tale to tell.

A Hebrew boy, child of a captive race,
   Snatched, at his birth, from Pharaoh's bloody hand,
Found, at the last, an unknown burial-place,
   In Moab's mountain land.

Yet all the kings that sat on Egypt's throne,
  Their glory, pomp and power combined in one,
Are poor and mean, forgotten and unknown,
  Measured with Amram's son.

In many climes, from east to utmost west,
  His stately name in shining glory stands;
And wider still, his spreading fame shall rest .
  O'er earth's far-lying lands.

The blind old man, who sang his wondrous song
  To Grecia's warlike tribes when Greece was young,
Whose echoing strains the ages yet prolong,
  In many a stranger tongue;

The high-browed Plato, crowned with heavenly light,
  Sitting as Master in the Academe,
Holding discourse of God and truth and right,
  And each divinest theme;

The strong souled Saxon, trusting God alone,
  Daring to stand for truth and liberty,
Hurling defiance at the papal throne,
  And setting nations free;

The full-orbed Shakespeare, with his radiant eye,
  Peering through peasant's cot and palace hall,
Ranging at will o'er earth and air and sky,
  At fancy's fairy call;

The men who sound the heavens and weigh the stars,
  And make safe pathways o'er the stormy deep,
Who gird the hill-tops with their iron bars,
  And bridge the mountain steep;

Who knit the world up with electric threads,
   That land may talk with land, as friend with friend,
Flashing their messages, on ocean beds,
   To earth's remotest ends;

Men of high action and of lofty thought,
   Whose words and deeds in living beauty shine,
While countless kings are buried and forgot,—
   These rule, by right divine.

CÆSAR AND CHRIST.

When Rome in her imperial pride,
   With conquering banners all unfurled,
Had spread her haughty conquests wide,
   And sat sole empress of the world;
Her dream was full—her throne at length
Seemed girt with universal strength.

On her seven hills, in glittering state,
   Temple and palace shine afar;
There dwell her mighty ones and great—
   Her nobles and her men of war;
And all her streets resound with mirth,
For Rome is mistress of the earth.

Far off, in Judah's captive land,
   Where bards and prophets once have trod,
There lingers yet a broken band—
   A race forsaken of its God;
But from this race a King shall rise
To sway all earthly destinies.

CÆSAR AND CHRIST.

The fulness of the time—foretold
   In vision, song, and prophecy,
By all the holy men of old—
   The fulness of the time draws nigh;
When Jacob's Star, with light divine,
O'er the bewildered race shall shine.

It was a night when earth was still;
   The heavens in silent splendor shone;
The winds breathed low on every hill,
   And stars looked down on mountain lone,
Till old Judea, rough and wild,
In strange and dreamy beauty smiled.

Away, amid the lonely hills,
   The gentle shepherds watched their sheep,
And heard the tinkling mountain rills
   Make music on the rocky steep;
Till on their ear, from heights above,
The angels poured their song of love.

This was that strange prophetic night,
   Dreamed of, through all the years of old,
When lawless Power should yield to Right,
   And earth should have its age of gold;
The rightful King should take the throne,
And shape an empire all his own.

This night, in Bethlehem's lowly shed,
   The Wonderful, The Counsellor,
The Prince of Peace, Earth's sovereign Head,
   Mightier than all her men of war,
Is born of woman—born to share
A human mother's love and care.

Afar, within Rome's iron walls,
   Men dream of empire as of old,
Through all her gay tumultuous halls
   Her lords their midnight revels hold:
Unknown to them this kingly birth,
Unknown this wonder of the earth.

The rolling centuries come and go,
   And Christ's dominion stretches on;
His empire, silently and slow,
   Rises o'er empires lost and gone;
His march is strong—his conquests sure—
His kingdom founded to endure.

Reign, reign, O King, with ampler power!
   Happy the land that feels thy sway!
Bring in that bright and joyous hour,
   When earth thy sceptre shall obey!
When heathen tribes, in gladsome awe,
And sea-girt isles, shall own thy law,

THE BATTLE OF THE WILDERNESS.

A MAIDEN is pacing her lonely room,
   In the midnight dark and deep,
The earth seems drear and sad as the tomb,
As she glances outward into the gloom,
   And her eyes can know no sleep.

Maiden, this is the month of May,
    And the earth is soft and green,
The whispering winds with the leaflets play,
And the birds with songs will welcome the day,
    And dance in its morning sheen.

Deeper and darker waxes the night,
    What cares she for May with its bloom?
Her eyes are filled with a strange, strange light,
And she looks far off with a yearning sight,
    Through the thick enveloping gloom.

Maiden, think not thou art watching alone,
    For thousands their vigils keep,
Mothers and wives and maidens make moan,
Through the weary night, as they toss and groan,
    And their eyes can know no sleep.

For rumors are floating on all the air,
    Of armies along their way;
The noise of drums and the trumpet's blare,
Bid the gathering squadrons haste and prepare
    To join in the dreadful fray.

And the letters have ceased—these heralds of love,
    That came from the quiet camp;
Coming as angels come from above,
Missives borne home as on wings of the dove
    To be read by the midnight lamp.

And tidings have come with the lightning's flash,
    They reached us at set of the sun,
Of the bold advance and the martial dash,
Of the mighty roar and the terrible crash
    Of the battle already begun.

THE BATTLE OF THE WILDERNESS.

The mustering hosts have passed out of our sight,
    To the depth of the Wilderness' shade,
To join in that long but victorious fight,
Though it shake the broad land with fear and affright,
    Making hearts that are stoutest afraid.

O maiden, look not from the window again,
    But wait for the breaking of day;
Thine eyes, they are weary with watching and pain;
They are restless and wild, and thou lookest in vain
    For thy lover so far away.

Can a maiden's heart rest, when her fears are awake
    For one who is dearer than life?
For one, whose courage no danger can shake,
Who has counted the cost and set life on the stake,
    And will be in the thick of the strife?

Ah maiden, 'tis well that weak is thy sight,
    For thy lover lies dead on the ground;
The armies file by in the shadows of night,
To give battle again with the dawning of light,
    But he heeds not the tumult around.

God pity thee, maiden, and list to thy cry,
    When the messenger comes to thy door,   [die,
For the young men must fall, and the young men must
With none bending o'er them to catch the last sigh
    Or give ear to the words they implore.

And pity the mothers and maidens afar,
    Who must weep and lament for the slain,
For war plants many a horrible scar,
Amid mountains and vales, far away from the jar
    And the smoke of the battle-plain.

EARTH'S WONDERS.

WHY must I roam the earth afar,
    And toil through distant lands,
Beneath the soft Italian star;
    Across Egyptian sands;
To trace the ravages of war,
    And wrecks of human hands?

The grandest sights earth has to show,
    Stand wide for you and me;
The mightiest wonders here below,
    God's children all may see,
As on their daily paths they go,
    With spirits glad and free.

Go climb the nearest mountain height,
    And watch the sun's decline:
Mark how the colored bars of light
    On Summer landscapes shine;
Till meadows glow with radiance bright,
    With splendors half divine.

Go see the full moon, calm and still,
    On autumn valleys rest;
Her dreamy veil thrown round the hill
    And lonely mountain crest,
Till earth is hushed to God's sweet will,
    And in His smile is blest.

Why must I seek the ruined heaps
    Which groaning captives piled;
Where musing memory sits and weeps
    And mercy never smiled;
And where stern desolation keeps
    Her empire strange and wild?

I lose myself in shady nooks,
    To watch the ways of God;
To read fair Nature's open books
    In cloisters seldom trod,
With music from the running brooks,
    And winds that stir abroad.

What though I never shall behold
    The realms of ancient skill;
The mighty palaces of old,
    On many a lordly hill;
Temples bedecked with stolen gold,
    To please some tyrant's will?

I've seen the march of breaking day,
    With cloudy banners bright;
I've seen Orion on his way,
    Along the fields of light;
And fiery streamers dance and play
    Above the Arctic night.

There is no charm of joy that springs
    From man's laborious art,
To touch the soul's most secret strings
    And soothe the restless heart,
Like that sweet calm which Nature brings,
    And God's great works impart.

Then if I tread no foreign strand,
    And see no alien sky,
But linger in my native land
    Until the day I die,
God's works and wonders, high and grand,
    Have passed before mine eye.

THE HOUSE BY THE SEA.

In our lonely home the fire burns bright,
    And the shadows play on the wall,
But there's trouble abroad on the sea to-night,
    And none can answer its call;
In the lull of the wind, we hear from the shore
    The mighty swing of the sea,
As it breaks, with its strange tumultuous roar,
    In its awful majesty.

All day, in our ears, the sighing blast
    Has told of the gathering storm,
And now, with the night, it comes at last
    In its wildest, fearfullest form:
The heavens are filled with the whirling snow,
    And the sea-spray rides on the gale,
While the tempest dirges come and go
    Like a sad funereal wail.

We think, as we watch the flickering flame,
    Of a night in the years gone by,
When out of the howling darkness came
    A sad and pitiful cry:
As we hurried apace to the sounding shore,
    That cry on the wind went past,
A moment heard, then lost in the roar
    Of a louder, angrier blast.

O God! how weak is a human hand
    When thy winds are abroad in their might!
When thou ridest in storm over ocean and land,
    Pavilioned in tempest and night!
There came, once again, on the wings of the gale,
    A loud and more desolate cry,
And it needed no more to tell us the tale
    Of man, in his agony.

In our lonely home the fire burns bright,
    And the shadows play on the wall;
But pity the sailor-boys struggling to-night
    Where none can answer their call.
What hand can be strong, what heart can be bold,
    When the midnight hurricane raves?
O pity the sailor-boys, hungry and cold,
    Who fight with these tempest-tost waves.

TOIL AND REST.

" For so He giveth His beloved sleep."

WHEN sets the weary sun,
And the long day is done,
And starry orbs their solemn vigils keep;
When bent with toil and care,
We breathe our evening prayer,
God gently giveth His belovéd sleep.

When by some slanderous tongue
The heart is sharply stung,
And with the sense of cruel wrong we weep;
How like some heavenly calm,
Comes down the soothing balm,
What time He giveth His belovéd sleep.

O sweet and blessèd rest,
With these sore burdens pressed,
To lose ourselves in slumbers, long and deep;
To drop our heavy load
Beside the dusty road,
When He hath given His belovéd sleep.

And on our closéd eyes
What visions may arise,
What sights of joy to make the spirit leap,
What memories may return,
From out their golden urn,
If God but giveth His belovéd sleep!

And when life's day shall close
In death's last deep repose,
When the dark shadows o'er the eyelids creep;
Let us not be afraid,
At this thick gathering shade,
For so God giveth His belovéd sleep.

To sleep?—it is to wake,
When the fresh day shall break,
When the new sun climbs up the eastern steep;
To wake with new-born powers,
Out from these darkened hours,
For so He giveth his belovéd sleep.

To die? it is to rise
To fairer, brighter skies,
Where Death no more shall his dread harvests reap;
To soar on angel wings,
Where life immortal springs,
For so He giveth His belovéd sleep.

THE GREAT CITY AT MIDNIGHT.

A voice of weeping and of lamentation,
   From the great city, with its shame and sin;
The wail of souls, that feel their degradation,
   All that they are, and all they might have been.

In the deep silence of their midnight waking,
   When left alone with Conscience and their God,
They mourn the hour, when Heaven's kind voice forsaking,
   They left the paths their early feet have trod.

In haunts of vice, in prisons cold and dreary,
   In vile abodes where guilt and horror reign,
How many wretched spirits, worn and weary,
   Drag out the night in fear and hopeless pain!

Their thoughts go back to the old vales and mountains,
   To happy homes amid green fields afar,
When they went wandering by the hill-side fountains,
   And hope rose in them like the morning star.

O wretched souls!—if once they look before them,
   They see a future, wild and tempest tost;
And looking backward, busy thoughts come o'er them
   Of the fair heritage their sin has lost.

Is there a balm to heal the broken spirit?
   Is there a cure for sin's most deadly blight?
This cry of souls—O God in Heaven, hear it,
   And draw them out of darkness into light.

THE TWO SONGS.

Two songs go up forever from the earth:
One the full choral swell of joy and gladness;
The other is a strain unknown to mirth,
The low, sad wail of mortal grief and sadness.
Turn where we may,—in lands afar or near,
These songs of joy and woe are still ascending;
Voices of love, and hope, and gladsome cheer
With notes of sorrow are forever blending.

Here ruddy health goes singing on its way;
There the pale sufferer on his couch is lying;
Here the glad shout of children at their play;
There the sharp farewell cries about the dying:
Here a fond mother walking in the light,
Because her darling son has come to honor;
And there a mother, sobbing out the night,
Whose darling son has brought disgrace upon her.

Hark, the glad music on the morning air,
When the sweet summer day is just awaking;
And hark afar, those accents of despair
On the wild shores where stormy waves are breaking.
Here rings aloud the merry marriage bell,
And some fair bride goes with her maids attended;
And there is tolling the sad funeral knell,
As some young, happy mother's life is ended.

Such are the songs that echo o'er the earth;
Our pathway now in light,—now sad and dreary;
The hours of grief press close the hours of mirth,
And happy days give place to days aweary:
But in the habitations of the blest,
In that fair land beyond the gloomy river,
The tiréd soul shall find its long-sought rest,
And the glad songs of joy go up forever.

WHO SAW THE STAR?

Who, of earth's dwellers, saw the wondrous star,
    Gilding the heavens on that mysterious night,
Lighting Judea's hill-tops from afar,
    And flooding Bethlehem with its mystic light?

Who heard, with awe-struck souls, the angel choirs
    Pouring their strains from unseen heights above,
Winging to earth, on their seraphic lyres,
    That marvellous song of peace and heavenly love?

Who saw and heard? Not the great ones and proud,
    Busy in search of power and fame and gold;
With thoughts cast down, a mad and restless crowd,
    They sought their low-born pleasures, as of old.

Not haughty monarchs in their lordly pride,
    Sitting enthroned in palaces of state,
Dreaming to stretch their empire far and wide,
    And bind the nations fast in chains of hate.

That herald light, the lonely shepherds see,
  Watching their flocks amid the silent hills,
With sleeping sheep, with stars for company,
  And tinkling music from the mountain rills.

That choral strain, unknown to monarch's ear,
  Unheard amid the stir and noise of earth,
Heaven's loving anthem, simple shepherds hear
  And learn the marvel of Emmanuel's birth.

God loves the gentle shepherds. He of old
  Called Amram's son, from keeping of the sheep,
Brought him afar from Horeb's desert fold,
  To lead his chosen tribes across the deep.

When Jesse's first born sons, with eager joy,
  Warlike and strong before the prophet stand,
Their dreams are vain; the ruddy shepherd boy
  Goes from the fold to Israel's high command.

So on that night when Bethlehem's star arose,
  Kings knew not what was passing on the earth;
To humble shepherds, hovering angels chose
  To tell the secret of the marvellous birth.

Earth's mighty centuries have rolled away,
  Since that strange orb arose to gild the night,
And many kings have lived their little day,
  And many empires vanished from the sight.

But Bethlehem's lowly babe, no more unknown,
  Before the world in form majestic stands,
Claims the wide earth for empire, all His own,
  With subjects countless as the countless sands.

EVENING AT CAPE ANN.

So sinks the peaceful day;
The weary sun goes down to glorious rest,
And fleecy clouds, in burning splendor drest,
    Hang round his shining way.

Gently comes in the night;
Softly her silent shadows are unrolled,
Till vale and hill, wrapt in her sombre fold,
    Fade from our mortal sight.

On this wild shore, alone,
Where storm-torn cliffs o'erhang the spreading sea,
And where the swinging tides, unceasingly,
    Make their low wailing moan,

I watch the opening sky,
Through which the stars come peering, one by one,
Their orbs unveiling, as the lordly sun
    Lays his dominion by.

And now heaven's glorious arch
Is set at last, in all its bright array;
The starry host, along its ancient way,
    Takes its majestic march.

'Tis good, in this still hour,
To gaze and dream—to sit in quiet thought,
Amid the marvellous wonders God has wrought,
    And feel their silent power.

EVENING AT CAPE ANN.

On such a night, of old,
The shepherd-bard of Judah kept his sheep,
And while the weary flock lay down to sleep,
    Safe sheltered in the fold,

His spirit rose on high,
To range the heavens and catch their mystic gleams,
While in the wanderings of his happy dreams,
    The wingèd hours flew by.

Firmly these heavens remain;
The earth rolls on with change and vexing wars,
But o'er the empire of the silent stars
    Quiet and order reign.

These starry orbs abide:
Arcturus still keeps watch above the north,
And arm'd Orion from the east comes forth,
    In his old warrior pride.

Now o'er the eastern wave,
Lo the round moon uprising from the sea!
Up the still heavens she rises, grand and free,
    From her low watery grave.

Along the unquiet deep,
She casts her solemn sheen of shivering light,
And gaining slowly her imperial height,
    Rules o'er the realms of sleep.

The soul in silent awe
Goes sounding through these boundless fields of space,
In search of that mysterious dwelling-place
    Where God sends forth his law.

O God! how frail is man!
Amid these distances and heights of power;
Measured as now, in this calm, thoughtful hour,
    With Thy far-reaching plan!

Yet in thine image made,
Man feels the throbbings of this boundless whole,
And whirling planets, as they nightly roll,
    Are in his balance weighed.

Give me a soul at peace,
Filled with the calm which rules these worlds above,
Till every thought shall bend in perfect love,
    And inward conflict cease!

SAINTLY WOMEN.

With gentle looks and hearts made calm by sorrow,
    I see them moving on their earthly way;
They wait, in patience, what may come to-morrow,
    Faithful to all the duties of to-day;
They watch around the bedside of the dying,
    And soothe the sufferers with their quiet cares,
They seek the homes where new-born grief is crying,
    And mingle service with their silent prayers.

The bloom of youth—the blush of early roses,
    Has faded, long ago, from off their cheek,
But in its stead, a holy peace reposes,
    A heavenly beauty, angel-like and meek:

The mirth and song—the choral of the dances—
    Have died away amid departed years,
The eyes look upward now, with loving glances,
    And death itself is shorn of all its fears.

It is the same old, ever-blessed story,
    Of holy women, clinging round the cross;
They had not seen the Lord's transfiguring glory,
    But they were with Him in His shame and loss:
Around His grave, with ointments and sweet spices,
    They hovered, as the birds about their nest;
For love like theirs dies not in cold surmises,
    But kindles courage in the humblest breast.

The costliest service human hands can render
    Comes without cost—is never bought and sold;
It flows from human hearts, by love made tender,
    And moves above the purchase-power of gold:
On the same paths where selfish greed is stalking,
    Rating all virtue at a market-price,
These saintly feet unselfishly are walking,
    To comfort pain and heal the wounds of vice.

Then tell me not that earth is wholly barren,
    While these angelic souls still linger here;
Sweeter than roses in the vale of Sharon,
    Are their kind deeds, besprinkled with a tear;
And heaven itself above their path is bending,
    To watch their acts of mercy, day by day,
And angel bands are on their steps attending,
    To shed a glory o'er their shining way.

A WINTER NIGHT.

A STRANGE enchantment fills the world;
  The winter winds are still;
A dreamy, mystic silence reigns
  O'er mountain, vale and hill:
The moon climbs up the eastern sky,
  In her full orb of light,
And looks, from deep and cloudless heavens,
  On boundless fields of white.

Fair as the bright and shining robes,
  In heavenly vision seen;
Pure as the vesture of the saints,
  That raiment white and clean;
So pure and fair these snowy folds,
  Fresh-woven from the skies,
That lend our lowly earth a grace
  Fit for angelic eyes.

How peacefully the shadows lie,
  All sloping to the west,
More beautiful than pictured forms
  By graver's art impressed!
Each twig upon the leafless tree,
  Each tendril of the vine,
Is caught by this fair tracery,
  In every bending line.

But sharp as is the icy breath
  That floats round Alpine heights;

A WINTER NIGHT.

Keen as the wind that chills the blood
   In lonely Arctic nights;
So keen and sharp this frosty air,
   This dense o'ermastering cold,
From which the muffled wanderer hastes
   To find some sheltering fold.

The night moves on, and one by one,
   The lamps, that lately shone,
Are quenched in farm-house and in cot,
   And moonlight reigns alone:
The last belated traveller
   Has hied him to his nest,
And not a sigh or sound disturbs
   This realm of perfect rest.

How many a wakeful eye to-night
   With light unwonted gleams!
How many a thoughtful soul is stirred
   With longing, happy dreams!
All that is good and pure within
   Is wakened into life,
And, like some far-off vision, fade
   All earthly sin and strife.

If God can make our world so fair,
   So pure before our eyes,
What shall the heavenly glory be
   Beyond these rolling skies?
If He can robe our sinful earth
   In such a spotless dress,
What shall the shining vesture be
   Of His own righteousness?

BUNKER HILL.

BRIEF was the summer night
On Bunker's busy height,
   One hundred years ago,
     In the leafy month of June;
When a thousand sturdy men,
From mountain, vale, and glen,
   Threw up their ramparts silently,
     Beneath the silent moon.

They had heard a warlike cry
Ring out along the sky,
   From Concord and from Lexington,
     That bloody April day;
And from many a lonely town
Strong men came hurrying down,
   Their muskets in their hands,
     To join the battle fray.

These are no hireling braves,
Like George's Hessian slaves,
   Coarse, mercenary outcasts,
     Who slaughter for their gain:
From quiet, happy homes
This patriot army comes,
   With weeping households left behind
     They ne'er may see again.

The dwellers by the sea,
The hardy men and free,
  Who brave the heaving ocean
    When eastern tempests roar,
Have left their boats to ride
Upon the swinging tide,
  Their little fishing smacks to rot
    Along the lazy shore.

The dwellers on the soil,
With arms made strong by toil,
  Have left their flocks untended,
    Their harvest fields unsown;
On many a lonely hill
The little farms lie still,
  The garden-lands and corn-lands
    With darnel overgrown.

This ringing call to war
Has sounded out afar,
  Down the New England valley,
    Along her western steep:
And o'er that northern land,
Where the grim mountains stand,
  Where the White Hills and the Green Hills
    Their solemn sentry keep.

It comes at last—the hour
When Britain's haughty power
  Shall learn, too late, how free-born men
    Will shake her ancient throne;

Will rend her galling chain,
And spurn her guiding rein,
　While she shall reap in sackcloth
　　The whirlwind she has sown.

　　＊　＊　＊　＊　＊　＊

A stir amid the fleet!
And a stir along the street!
　The hot and panting messengers
　　Are running to and fro;
The steeple-tops look down
On a bewildered town,
　And marvel at the tumult
　　That fills the world below.

With anger in his eye,
The chieftain gallops by,
　And waiting for his orders
　　The high subalterns stand;
He points to yonder height,
Which still defies his might,
　And wrath is burning through his words,
　　As he issues his command:

" What madness rules the hour!
Do they defy my power?
　These low-born rustics, will they dig
　　Their own ignoble graves!
Ring out the quick alarms
And call the men to arms;
　I'll drive them from their burrow
　　As the whirlwinds drive the waves.

"Summon the wandering boats!
Yea every barge that floats,
  And bear my trusty men across
    To storm yon rebel crest!
Come on, my Grenadiers!
With shoutings and with cheers,
  One look along your lines will fright
    These miscreants from their nest."

Sooth, 'twas a goodly sight,
This gathering for the fight,
  These firm-set ranks of Englishmen,
    In colors bright and gay;
With stars upon the breast,
With plume and nodding crest,
  How proudly to the battle
    They took their cheerful way!

But ye know not where ye go;
Ye have despised your foe;
  Pride walks before destruction,
    And swelling words are vain;
O turn and look once more
On hill and sea and shore,
  And catch this glorious sunlight
    Ye ne'er may see again!

If in your breast has stirred
Some kind and tender word,
  Go tell it to your messenger,
    To bear across the deep;

For ye are on your way
To death this very day,
 And in your far-off English homes
The loving ones must weep.

"I DWELL AMONG MINE OWN PEOPLE."

Nay, tempt me not, your words cannot avail;
 Speak not my name or deeds before the king;
I dwell with mine own people, in the dale,
 And do not wish the honors you would bring.

My people, rude of tongue, use honest speech;
 Untaught to please, they please by simple ways;
And their untutored language, each to each,
 Is nobler than all false and courtly phrase.

From the king's palace comes to me, afar,
 The sound of strife—a tumult and a noise,
The war of tongues—an endless, selfish jar.
 Shall I exchange for this my quiet joys?

With mine own people, though of humble lot,
 In sweet contentment do I choose to dwell;
All that the court can offer lures me not
 From these calm pleasures of my native dell:

For here I watch the early dawning light,
 And trace its kindling radiance on the hills,
And walk beneath the starry heavens at night,
 And hear the silver songs from mountain rills;

And singing birds make music on my way,
  And bright-eyed flowers spring up beneath my feet,
And sportive lambs along my pastures play,
  Or wondering flock about my grassy seat;

And ancient woods embrace me with their shade,
  And weave around me their undying charm;
Here I can walk, and never be afraid,
  Can ling r here, and dread no lurking harm.

But at the court, the arrow flies by day,
  And dread detraction wanders in the night,
And fierce revenge sits waiting for its prey,
  And justice sinks before the hand of might.

With mine own people then I choose to dwell,
  And leave the court to those who love its noise;
Name not my name—my deeds ye need not tell,
  I sit apart and love my simple joys.

THE SNOW-STORM.

In the early dawn of the morning,
  The skies began dropping their snow,
And the winds, through the forests, went singing
  That song which the winds only know;
But meanwhile the storm has been rising,
  And the mad winds sweep on in a gale,
They come from the fields of the ocean,
  And fill the wide land with their wail.

THE SNOW-STORM.

I sit at my study window,
    And look abroad on the world,
And watch while the fleecy snow-clouds
    On the wings of the wind are whirled:
My book lies idle before me,
    And I gaze, in a dreamy trance,
At the leaping, warping snow-flakes,
    As they move in their mystic dance.

Who knoweth the wonderful secret,
    The magical power of this spell?
What cunning pen can unfold it,
    Or what human tongue can tell?
This dreamy play of the fancy,
    As we gaze with steadfast eye,
On the cloudy, rolling tempest,
    Moving in tumult by?

Is the charm in the endless commotion,
    Like the march of a countless host?
Or when waves on waves come dashing
    On a wild far-reaching coast?
Do our wingèd thoughts leap upward,
    In search of that viewless form,
Who makes of the cloud His chariot,
    And rides on the wings of the storm?

But O, the Spirit within us!
    The harp with its mystical strings,
How Nature can wake it to music,
    With the breath of her fluttering wings!
Who knoweth the marvellous secret,
    The magical power of the spell?

What cunning pen can unfold it,
　Or what human tongue can tell?

Then blow, ye winds, from the ocean,
　With your weird and musical lay!
No more will I search for your secret,
　But yield myself up to your play;
My book lies idle before me,
　As I gaze, in a dreamy trance,
At the rolling, whirling snow-cloud,
　Moving in mystic dance.

THE MIDNIGHT TRAIN.

As I lay awake in the night,
　And heard the pattering rain,
Faintly I caught the rumbling sound
　Of the coming midnight train.

The world was murky and still,
　The air was loaded with damp,
And on the folds of the mist it came,
　The noise of this iron tramp;

Plunging through darkness and fog,
　Sending its signals before,
Searching the night with its eye of flame,
　And filling the earth with its roar.

I knew all the track, and could tell
   By the sinking and swell of the sound,
When it darted through woods, or climbed up a grade,
   Or leaped o'er a bridge at a bound.

Now the sound floated free on the air,
   Now it died round the curve of a hill,
Now lost to the ear in the deep rocky pass,
   But the mad thing was rushing on still;

Plunging through blackness and mist;
   Sending wild 'larums before;
Howling like demon of darkness let loose
   From Acheron's fiery shore.

And now all the windings are passed,
   And out it comes on to the plain,
Shaking the earth, as it tears along
   Through midnight blackness and rain.

O that some forest chief,
   From his ancient woodland nest,
Might peer through the night, and catch the wild sight
   Of this monster troubling his rest.

Nearer and nearer it comes,
   Louder the crash and the roar,
Bearing its precious load of life,
   Two hundred souls and more.

Many their errands be;
   Some journey for traffic and gain,
Some go to the gloomy chambers of death,
   And some to the bridal train.

Here are eyes heavy with sleep,
　　Here bright with the light of love,
In joy and in tears, with hopes or with fears,
　　On through the darkness they move.

And now it goes by with a leap,
　　Wild the weird flashes it throws,
Out of thick darkness it comes in its flight,
　　And into thick darkness it goes,—

Plunging through blackness and fog,
　　Sending loud signals before,
Searching the night with its eye of flame,
　　And filling the earth with its roar.

VANISHED FACES.

With shivering winds from the ocean,
　　And snow-flakes tossed in the blast,
The darkness came down, and the snow-clouds
　　Are whirling till midnight is past:
I linger in dreams by the fireside,
　　And watch o'er the embers at play,
As they gleam, in the lift of the tempest,
　　Or dusk, as the dirge dies away.

In visions come flitting before me
　　The days of the years that are dead;
The three-score years that are numbered,
　　And back to eternity fled:

VANISHED FACES.

At each step, at each turn of the journey,
   We have left our companions behind;
They dropt as the leaves of the autumn,
   And were hurried away with the wind.

The loved ones with whom we took counsel,
   Who walked with us once by the way,
How they throng in these watches of midnight,
   But are gone ere the breaking of day!
From the land of the mist and the shadow
   Their faces peer out to the light;
'Tis a look—'tis the glimpse of a moment,
   And they vanish again from our sight.

Though the vision vouchsafed may not tarry,
   Yet the dream and the vision are true;
We have seen with our eyes the departed,
   We have looked in their faces anew:
The mother, who watched by our cradle,
   The father, our glory and pride,
The maiden, whose eyes were love-lighted,
   And the comrades who walked by our side.

They were clad in the robes of the morning,
   Or the glow of the noontide sun,
Or they stood in the shadows of evening,
   As pilgrims whose journey was done:
We have seen them—their faces transfigured,
   And a mystical light on their head,
For the fleshly no more held dominion,
   And the earthly-born passions were dead.

O fair are the stars that besprinkle
   The fields of the heavenly space;
But fairer the radiance shining
   In a saintly and purified face;
So we sit by the flickering firelight,
   And watch the old faces come back,
They pass in a dreamy procession
   On their silent and shadowy track.

THE MAYFLOWER.

How dar'st thou try this stormy path,
   Thou frail and struggling bark!
Old England's shores are shut from sight
   Amid the gathering dark.
The friends, who waved their sad adieu,
   Have homeward gone to weep,
And thou art left, a lonely waif,
   Upon the boundless deep.

Night closes round thy little group
   Of aching, homesick hearts,
That strive to hide the thoughts which rise,
   And quench the tear that starts;
But hard it is, on wings of faith,
   To mount o'er present fears,
And see the glory that may break
   Around the distant years.

Yet sail thou on, thou shalt not fail
  To reach yon waiting shores;
Thou carriest treasures, costlier far
  Than Ophir's golden stores;
If Cæsar's bark must needs be safe
  Amid the angry waves,
The men thou bearest cannot sink
  In ocean's gloomy caves.

Sail gladly on, the world behind
  Is rent with hate and strife;
The canker of a thousand years
  Is feeding on its life;
Yea, welcome, as thy truest friend,
  This broad dividing sea;
Its stormy ramparts are thy shield,
  The world beyond is free.

The little seed, by Pilgrim hands,
  In fear and weakness sown,
May wait through long and weary years
  Before to fulness grown;
But it shall stand, a mighty tree,
  In glory and in pride,
And through the rising ages stretch
  Its fruitful branches wide.

Then sail thou on, though torn and tossed
  By tempests driven and hurled,
Thou hast the charter which shall shape
  And rule a coming world.

The tyrant kings, with haughty power,
    Who scorned thy low estate,
Shall roam as exiles in the earth,
    And on thy bidding wait.

Fair freedom from this hour shall date
    A new and wondrous birth;
The light of liberty shall rise
    To spread o'er all the earth;
The monarch's gilded throne shall grow
    A cheap and childish thing,
For man in dignity shall stand,
    And God alone be king.

Earth's ancient tribes and lands remote;
    Where Indus rolls his tides,
Or where the Northern dwellers climb
    The snowy mountain sides;
Where the fierce Arab spurs his steed
    Across the burning plain,
Or fur-clad Russians drive the deer
    With freely flowing rein;

Where the dark Ethiop spreads his tent
    On Afric's Eastern shores,
Or forest hunters skim the waves
    With lightly dipping oars,—
All lands beneath the circling sun,
    All islands of the sea,
As centuries roll shall taste the fruit
    From this fair Pilgrim tree.

RIPE FOR HEAVEN.

I know an aged pilgrim, worn and weary,
    Whose feet still linger on the sands of time;
But earth for him is all too cold and dreary,
    He longs to reach a sunnier, happier clime.

His eye is dim, his ear is dull of hearing,
    Old sights and sounds disturb his soul no more,
He sees the goodly hills, their crests uprearing,
    The sunlit hills upon the farther shore.

In his long journey o'er the desert ranges,
    His soul has known sharp conflicts by the way,
The fierce temptations, and the bitter changes,
    The chills of night, the burning heats of day.

But now he sits in patience by the river,
    Gentle and quiet as a weanèd child,
Waiting for God the summons to deliver,
    To call him up to mansions undefiled.

Ask him of human life, its plots and scheming,
    Its small ambitions and its empty joys;
He answers like a sleeper waked from dreaming,
    He lives afar from all this strife and noise.

But ask of Heaven, and of the joys that cluster
    Around that land where his Redeemer lives,
His fading eye lights up with heavenly lustre,
    And his quick tongue the ready answer gives.

DECEMBER 21ST,
1620–1870.

Ye children of New England,
  Wherever ye may be,
Whether ye keep the ancient homes
  Down by the ancient sea;
Treading the rocky pathways
  Your fathers trod before,
Hearing the wild Atlantic break
  Along her stormy shore;
Or if afar ye wander,
  O'er the prairies of the West,
Or down the wide Pacific slopes,
  Your weary footsteps rest:

Come listen to my story,
  The grand ancestral lay,
Which as the world grows older,
  Grows newer every day;
Which touches men with pity,
  And touches men with pride,
In the memory of those noble souls,
  For God who lived and died.

This is no play of fancy,
  To catch a listless ear;
No strange and shadowy legend,
  For idle minds to hear,

YE CHILDREN OF NEW ENGLAND.

No tale of love and sorrow,
   To rob the eye of sleep
O'er which pale sickly maidens
   May weep and read and weep.

'Tis a tale of faith and patience,
   And a tale of cruel wrong,
When the good to earth were trampled,
   By the haughty and the strong;
The brave, heroic Pilgrims
   Could find no place of rest,
Save o'er the stormy ocean,
   In the forests of the West.

Behold these storm-tost Pilgrims,
   On a rough and barren shore;
With the sounding sea behind them,
   And the wilderness before;
Hungry and cold they house them
   In their dwellings rude and low,
While the night winds howl around them
   With their drifting clouds of snow.

In these nights of care and watching,
   Long nights unblest with sleep,
What strange fantastic terrors,
   Over the spirits creep!
Out from these unknown forests,
   Come stealing on the ear,
Weird and mysterious voices,
   That chill the soul with fear.

Oh the terrors of that winter,
    When men sickened day by day,
And one by one, as weeks rolled on,
    They dropt and passed away!
There was no harsh and murmuring voice,
    No sad complaining cry,
But silently they heard the call
    And laid them down to die.

Meekly as to the slaughter
    The patient lamb is led,
Meekly before her shearers
    As the sheep bows down her head;
So bowed these humble Pilgrims
    Before the chastening rod,
And opened not their mouth, to doubt
    The goodness of their God.

Strong men and gentle women,
    The maiden in her bloom,
The little child, the grey-haired sire,
    Slept in their hill-side tomb;
They were buried there in darkness,
    And the living smoothed their bed,
That the fierce savage might not tell
    The number of the dead.

And when the genial sun came back,
    And these dark months were o'er,
When through the budding forests,
    The soft winds blew once more,

Half of their number could not feel
　Its sweet reviving breath,—
They slept upon the burial hill
　The icy sleep of death.

But these days of fiery trial,
　Of scorn and hate, are o'er,
And now these grand old Pilgrim sires
　Shall live to die no more;
Men kindle at their virtues,
　They tell with swelling pride
The story of those men of old,
　For God who lived and died.

And as the years roll onward,
　Through the ages yet to be,
As wider grows and wider;
　This empire of the free;
Grander shall grow the story
　Of those men, true and tried,
Those noble and heroic souls,
　For God who lived and died,

PLYMOUTH AND THE BAY.

THEY tell of the mighty founders,
    And the empires great of old,
Of the rough gigantic Nimrod,
    And of Romulus the bold,
Of the fierce barbaric warriors,
    And the pirates of the flood,
Who built their thrones by plunder,
    And stained their courts with blood:
But we sing, in a grander story,
    Of the men who crossed the sea,
To change these western forests
    To an empire of the free;
The hand of the Lord was with them,
    Along their perilous way,
And they laid their firm foundations
    At Plymouth and the Bay.

They would not bend the conscience
    To suit a tyrant's frown,
And at the feet of haughty kings
    They would not bow them down;
They met their proud oppressors
    With calm undaunted eye,
As men long used to suffer,
    And not afraid to die;
In the strength of God they trusted,
    In the love of God they wrought,

PLYMOUTH AND THE BAY.

Nor gold, nor earthly glory,
   Nor praise of men, they sought.
In humble faith and patience
   They lived their little day,
And laid their strong foundations
   At Plymouth and the Bay.

And now, when generous harvests
   Have all been gathered in,
And full, ripe, yellow ears of corn
   Press the well-loaded bin;
When the sharp chilly north wind
   With a wild song hurries past,
And the fallen leaves are whirling
   Before the fitful blast;
When on the well-swept hearthstones
   The fires are burning bright,
And children gather homeward
   With merry hearts and light,
We keep our glad Thanksgiving
   In memory of that day
Kept by the brave old Founders
   At Plymouth and the Bay.

Mean was their earthly treasure,
   And small their harvest store,
But they blessed the faithful Giver,
   And did not covet more;
They sat in their rude dwellings,
   Close by the stormy sea,
Rejoicing most of all that now
   Their weary souls were free.

Let men shoot out their arrows,
And wing their words of hate,
They only show their little minds
And their own mean estate:
The good, the noble of the earth,
Will their glad homage pay
To the men who laid foundations
At Plymouth and the Bay.

A PILGRIM FATHER RECONSTRUCTED.

FOREFATHERS' DAY.—CONGREGATIONAL CLUB.
1880.

THE wandering sun, ranging through southern skies,
Has touched his wintry solstice. O'er the north
Fall the chill shadows, and the sickly days,
Pale-faced and wan, are quickly lost in night.
From the cold heavens, through lonely midnight hours,
The glittering stars look down on fields of ice,
On plains and mountains wrapped in robes of snow.
Along the headlands of our rock-bound coast
The wild waves roll, and the hoarse murmurs break,
Telling the lonely dwellers by the sea
Of far-off winds and storms and tossing barks.

RECONSTRUCTED PILGRIM.

Now is the midnight of our northern year:
Nature has laid aside her flowery robes,
And clothed herself in soberest attire.
All sights and sounds, in earth and air and heaven,
Recall those stern historic days of old,
When our brave Pilgrim sires, battling with waves,
Struggling with icy winds and adverse fate,
Made their rude entry on these western shores.
Now, in our well-filled homes, by genial fires,
We read the tale,—tell o'er the honored names,
Those grand and simple names that cannot die,
And proudly trace our ancient lineage."

We read the critics too, those sharp-eyed men,
Who search all precious ointments through and through,
Not for the ointment's sake, to prove its worth,
But, if so be, to find out and report
Some smallest fly that may have lodged therein.
Our Pilgrim critics are an ancient brood,
Hovering about the rock from age to age,
With nods portentous, and with croaking voice.
'Tis well to read these critics—well to know
Their inmost thought, and follow where they lead.
Guided by them, and walking in their light,
Let us now reconstruct our Pilgrim sires,
And show what men our fathers should have been.

The Pilgrim Father should have been a man,
  Who had no private prejudice to smother,
Built on a large, expansive, liberal plan,
  To whom one thing were good as any other;

Who, had he lived back when the race began,
    Would not have minded when Cain killed his brother;
A man so very round and full and pious
As to be free from every shade of bias.

He should have patronized with equal zeal
    Every adventurous and random rover;
Have freely shared his dear-bought common weal
    With every renegade that might come over;
Ready to grant each wanderer's appeal,
    Whether he came from Holland, Dublin, Dover;
A man who held it strict impartiality
Not to distinguish virtue from rascality.

Once here, our Pilgrim's first and foremost thought
    Ought to have been to please his Indian neighbor;
What though the cunning, lazy savage sought
    To gain his living without care or labor;
Still, our good Pilgrim ought not to have brought
    To this new world his musket and his sabre;
It surely was not generous and good
To frighten these poor children of the wood.

They were the dwellers on this Western soil,
    Centuries before the Mayflower went a-cruising;
If they preferred to live exempt from toil,
    Who had the right to hinder them from choosing?
Or, if they forced their wives to slave and moil,
    Beating or killing any one refusing,
The Pilgrim Father was a stranger here,
What arrogance in him to interfere!

He should have landed on this Western shore
  With less of Bible, and with more of science;
Bible is good, but had he pondered o'er
  What science taught, and made that his reliance,
He could have reared, from his exhaustless store,
  An empire grand, and bid the world defiance:
Great pity that with chances so prodigious
He should have been a trifle too religious.

Given, just scientific lore enough
  Simply to analyze that famous boulder
Called Plymouth Rock, where "breaking waves dashed"— rough—
  That rock which thrills with awe each new beholder:
Given, the mica, quartz, and other stuff
  Employed and used by the primeval molder
To forge, by aid of underground caloric,
That marvellous rock now grown to be historic;

Given, the power to tell, like modern sages,
  Somewhere within five hundred thousand years
How old that boulder is, and what the stages
  By which it journeyed to these Plymouth piers;
To trace its starting-point in by-gone ages,
  And show how easy everything appears:
Items like these are solid information,
Well fitted to build up a mighty nation.

But we go prating on about this rock,
  Its mental, moral and religious uses?
We treat it like some huge æsthetic block,
  Whose very name to boundless good conduces:

We feel a kind of sentimental shock
   When any scoffer offers his abuses:
From sixteen hundred twenty to this day,
The rock has served in this peculiar way.

Here endeth the first lesson. Turn the page,
   And we may find all freshly spread before us
The counter-charges of a later age
   Which may, by contrast, comfort and restore us.
Critics in war with critics will engage
   Long as the centuries go rolling o'er us;
If we could tarry till their strife were ended,
Our Pilgrim sires would surely be defended.

These counter-charges which we have in hand
   Seem, in their contrasts, just a little funny.
The Pilgrims, now, are not a pious band;
   They came, it seems, intent on making money.
They fancied that this rough New-England land
   Might prove to them a land of milk and honey;
And so they ventured o'er a stormy ocean
To pay, at Mammon's shrine, their pure devotion.

They were a wandering clan, that could not rest
   Or live contented in their own condition;
And when they left their ancient English nest,
   They only showed their restless disposition;
Ready to journey east or journey west,
   Upon their money-making expedition;
They tried old Holland, and, ignobly failing,
Away to Plymouth Rock they went a-sailing.

But know ye well, Oh critics, ye spend your strength for nought;
All harmless fall the weapons your cunning hands have wrought;
The men ye seek to injure have reached a height sublime,
Whereon they sit secure against the accidents of time:
The rolling years have tried them, the centuries have passed,
And clothed them with a glory that shall forever last.

The wandering birds that fly afar are wise to know their hour; . [power,
Seeking the fields of upper air, and thwarting human
They voyage on unguided by compass or by chart,
Along these clear and azure heights, safe from the hunter's dart;
A law they know not moves them straight to their distant nest,
Unerringly they journey and find their promised rest.

So the old patriarchs journeyed, moved by the call of God, [trod:
Earth's wanderers, unknowing the pathway which they
And so the Pilgrims journeyed, leaving their native land,
Going they knew not whither, by some divine command;
With faith and loving patience they trod their weary way, [day.
And so their names stand glorified before our eyes to—

The best and purest wisdom is wisdom of the heart,
Untouched by human cunning, unstained by earthly art;
He that by craft will save his life shall lose it at the end,
He that will lose his life shall find an everlasting friend:
God has his chosen children, his favorites on the earth,
Raised out of toil and sorrow by an immortal birth.

THE BEWILDERED PROPHET.

"I shall see him, but not now."

It is sure, and mine eye shall behold him,
    But not in these days that are nigh;
The years afar off shall unfold him,
    When the cycles of time have gone by:
Then the star shall gleam out in its splendor,
    The star that from Jacob shall rise;
And Israel's strength and defender
    Shall appear from His throne in the skies.

But first must come travail and labor,
    And first must come sorrow and toil,
For the mountains of Sinai and Tabor
    Must shed down their wealth on the soil:
It is certain—the dream and the vision,
    When the ages of trial are past,
For it waits—in the Vale of Decision,
    It shall come, in its fulness, at last.

From the top of the rocks I espy him,
    Through the mist and the cloud he appears,
From the height of the hills I descry him,
    Far adown through the shadowy years;

And below, in the beautiful valley,
    The white tents of Jacob are spread;
Who can number the hosts as they rally?
    Who can look on their strength without dread?

Surely God is upholding the nation,
    And guarding its marvellous birth,
He has fixed and determined its station,
    Alone, 'mid the tribes of the earth;
And my curse has returned to a blessing,
    And my tongue, that was strong, is made weak,
And I come, in my struggle, confessing
    That I know not the words which I speak.

How goodly thy tents by the river!
    How fair thy pavilions outspread!
And can I my message deliver,
    And pour out a curse on thy head?
The vision is sure—I behold him,
    But not in these days that are nigh,
The years afar off shall unfold him,
    And the star shall gleam out in the sky.

"TELL ABOUT."

I know a fair-haired child, with shining eyes,
    Whose little feet go pattering in and out,
Seeking for some one who will make her wise,
    Her every question ending, "Tell about."

"TELL ABOUT."

Her new-found world is like some fairy land,
    All wonderful, but shadowed o'er with doubt;
And so she turns for light on every hand,
    And will her friends just please to "tell about"?

When grass grows green, and flowers begin to spring,
    And birds are singing in the world without,
Her airy fancies rise on playful wing,
    These sights and sounds some one must "tell about."

With picture-book in hand, her busy feet
    From room to room at last have found you out,
And on your knee she asks to take a seat,
    While this loved volume will you "tell about"?

When God and heaven are mentioned in her ear,
    She stands with looks half-wondering and devout,
She knows not whether they be far or near,
    But looking up she whispers, "Tell about."

We are but children of a larger age,
    And better taught how little we can know,
And as we study Nature's wondrous page
    Our restless thoughts go wandering to and fro.

The mystery of earth and air and sea,
    The sky bestud with burning worlds of light,
Of time in all its past eternity,
    And all the ranges of its future flight:

The mystery of God, and life, and death,
    The world within us and the world without,
Before them all we stand with bated breath,
    Waiting for some one who will "tell about."

HEAVEN IS FAR AND EARTH IS NEAR.

When first the soul, on joyous wings,
    Mounts up and takes its heavenward way,
Like the glad lark it soars and sings
    Before the shining gates of day;
It seems set free from earthly thralls,
    From its old bondage-house of fear;
But ah, how soon it faints and falls,
    For heaven is far and earth is near!

Often we gain some lofty height,
    Some mount of God, serene and still,
Where shines a pure transfiguring light,
    And holy thoughts like dews distil;
And here, we dream, shall be our stay,
    We'll build our tabernacles here;—
Alas, these visions glide away,
    For heaven is far and earth is near!

So Bunyan's pilgrims toiled of old,
    Up to the mountain-tops of rest,
And saw afar the streets of gold,
    Saw the bright mansions of the blest;
And from these heights of sweet content,
    Where all around was calm and clear,
Down to the vales of sense they went,
    For heaven is far and earth is near.

O mystery of earth and sin!
    This war forever round the soul!
I find a law of God within,
    But the old law will still control;
I will to do, and do it not,
    For earth-born passions interfere;
I struggle upward in my thought,
    But heaven is far and earth is near.

"We walk by faith and not by sight,"
    And faith is weak and sight is strong;
We choose the good, approve the right,
    And wander blindly to the wrong;
O soul, still driven and tempest-tost,
    'Mid good and evil, hope and fear!
Christ will not leave thee to be lost,
    Though heaven is far and earth is near.

"THEY THAT WATCH FOR THE MORNING."

EARTH lies in shadows: wanderers of the night,
We walk amid a dim uncertain light,
Waiting the hour, when on our eager sight
    Shall break the radiant morn.

"THEY THAT WATCH FOR THE MORNING."

Lost in the gloom, our feet have strayed afar;
Our path is hid; we know not where we are.
Oh, for the rising of that herald star
    Which ushers in the morn!

Far off, we hear the lonely mountain rill,
While dews of night fall on us; and a chill
Comes creeping in the shadows of the hill;
    We watch and wish for morn.

Strange voices reach us from the forest shade,
Strange unknown sounds, that make our souls afraid;
We move in silence, trembling and dismayed,
    Yearning to hail the morn.

Fear gives our wild bewildered fancies play, [way—
And phantom forms throng round our darksome
Spectres, that vanish with the light of day,
    The dawning of the morn.

And now the lightning gleam goes flashing by;
Low muttering thunder stirs the western sky.
Oh for some refuge, where our feet may fly,
    And wait the coming morn!

When, when shall we arise and night be gone?
When shall these gloomy shadows be withdrawn,
And on us burst the effulgence of the dawn,
    The bright immortal morn?

Oh, joy to reach that land, which knows no night,
To stand, at last, on that celestial height
Where God shall be our everlasting light.
    Break, break, thou heavenly morn!

THE UNKNOWN LAND.

O LAND unknown! Beyond our mortal sight,
Wrapt round with gloomy shadows of the night;
Our spirits dread, yet long to wing their flight
    To thy mysterious shores.

O land unknown! We strain our eager eye;
Into the dark we send our pleading cry;
We call in vain; no voices make reply
    From thy mysterious shores.

O land unknown! A never-ending train
In stern procession from these realms of pain,
Moves slowly on, but comes not back again
    From thy mysterious shores.

O land unknown! Art thou far off, or near?
We only know our loved ones disappear,
And the old voices we no more can hear
    From thy mysterious shores.

O land unknown! By the dividing stream
We stand and gaze, and sometimes fondly dream
The clouds will part and yield one transient gleam
    Of thy mysterious shores.

O land unknown! That day of days draws nigh,
Which shall unlock this hidden mystery,
And bid our dreading, longing spirits fly
    To thy mysterious shores!

THE FIRST THANKSGIVING.
1621.

EDWARD WINSLOW'S STORY.

WE had gathered in our harvests,
    And stored the yellow grain,
For God had sent the sunshine,
    And sent the plenteous rain;
Our barley-land and corn-land
    Had yielded up their store,
And the fear and dread of famine
    Oppressed our homes no more.

As the chosen tribes of Israel,
    In the far years of old,
When the summer fruits were garnered,
    And before the winter's cold,
Kept their festal week with gladness,
    With songs and choral lays,
So we kept our first thanksgiving
    In the hazy autumn days.

Through the mild months of summer,
    We had built us pleasant homes,
So that now we fear no danger,
    When the angry winter comes;

THE FIRST THANKSGIVING.

We can sit by cheerful firesides,
  And watch the flickering ray,
When the storms of ocean gather,
  And howl around the bay.

We think with grief and sadness,
  Of the gloomy months gone by,
When want was in our dwellings,
  And we saw our loved ones die;
But when our well-filled garners
  Moved all our hearts to praise,
We kept our glad thanksgiving
  In the soft October days.

We sent our keen-eyed gunners
  To the forest-haunts for game;
And with ample wealth of wild-fowl,
  Rejoicing home they came;
And our good Indian neighbors,
  With whom we live in peace,
Brought in their gift of hunted deer,
  Our larder to increase.

And Massasoit, the chieftain,
  Was present with us then;
He came to share our banquet,
  With his ninety dusky men;
So for three days we feasted,
  With sports and games and plays,
And kept our first thanksgiving
  In the fair autumnal days.

The winds breathed gently on us,
  From out the mild southwest;

THE FIRST THANKSGIVING.

They come, the Indians tell us,
   From the islands of the blest;
And the sun and moon looked kindly
   From the still heights above,
As if to cheer our banquet,
   And bless our feast of love.

And our brave Captain Standish,
   Brought up 'mid war's alarms,
Led out his small but trusty band,
   His sturdy men at arms;
He showed the Indian warriors
   Our military ways,
For so we kept thanksgiving
   In those lazy autumn days.

We thought of dear old England,
   Dear, though to us unkind;
Of the fond familiar faces,
   That we had left behind;
But England cannot wean us
   Back from our forest home,
Where we lay our sure foundations
   For the better years to come.

So we passed the days in gladness,
   In social joy and mirth,
As those who have their dwelling-place
   As yet upon the earth;
But to the Lord our God, we brought
   Our gifts of prayer and praise;
So we kept our first thanksgiving
   In the dreamy autumn days.

THE MYSTERY OF THE STARS.

When night, that veils the earth, unveils the sky,
And opens worlds unnumbered to the eye,
　　Kindling with light the spreading vault o'er-arching;
The starry groups which stud the heavenly space,
That shone on patriarchs of the early race,
Are shining yet, and with majestic pace
　　Along their ancient pathways still are marching.

Orion, in the clear autumnal nights,
Comes proudly climbing up the eastern heights,
　　His silvery bands in all their beauty gleaming;
Arcturus greets us with his shining face,
The Pleiades still wear their native grace,
The North Star hangs above " the empty place,"
　　Where the mysterious Arctic fires are streaming.

But, oh, what thought can sound these boundless deeps,
Where awful silence her grim empire keeps,
　　And where the worlds on fiery wheels are speeding?
With wondering, longing eyes we stand and gaze,
With seers and sages of primeval days,
And while our hearts go out in hymns of praise,
　　Our inmost souls for light, for light are pleading.

How lone and desolate these fields of air,
Except an ever-living God be there

To rule and guide through all these boundless ranges:
A King, with power to act a kingly part,
A heavenly Father with a father's heart,
To feel His children's every grief and smart,
  And bear them up through all life's weary changes.

If, on the wings of morning, we can rise,
And range the outmost limits of the skies,
  Where the long wandering stars are homeward wheeling,
And feel that God attends us on our flight,
These dreary solitudes are filled with light,
The heavens and earth are but a mirror bright,
  God's greatness, wisdom, power and love revealing.

CHRISTIAN OLD AGE.

WHY should we longer wait?
These mortal years grow weary in their round;
They wheel and roll, from goal to outmost bound,
With one recurring tide of sight and sound,—
    Why should we wait?

Why should we longer wait?
The shifting seasons still will come and go,
The sun will scorch in summer—and the snow
Will load the air, what time the north winds blow,—
    Why should we wait?

Why should we longer wait?
The things that are, are things that have gone by,
There are no wonders more of earth or sky;
Let us depart—the time has come to die,—
    Why should we wait?

Why should we longer wait?
Around us breaks the old unceasing din,
The empty war of selfishness and sin; [win,—
Groans from the fallen—shouts from those who
    Why should we wait?

Why should we longer wait?
The senses move within a narrow bound,
We catch dim glimpses of a world around,
And life goes on like some confusing sound,—
    Why should we wait?

Why should we longer wait?
For earth-born hopes no more can have their play,
In lonely nights, we wait the breaking day,
Nor do we wish the morning hours to stay,—
    Why should we wait?

Why should we longer wait?
Those we have loved have journeyed on before;
They wait our coming on the further shore,
And Earth is vacant for us, evermore,—
    Why should we wait?

Let us arise and go!
The night is well-nigh spent—the day at hand!
We catch some whisperings from that other land,
We hear the music from some angel-band,—
    Let us arise!

Let us arise and go!
All that we are to Christ our Lord belongs,
And we would join with the unnumbered throngs,
That girt his throne with everlasting songs,—
    Let us arise!

Let us depart from hence!
We have outlived our little earthly day;
All things are ready—we would flee away
Unto that land, where sin has no more sway,—
    Let us depart!

THANKSGIVING.

The daylight hours grow brief and dim,
    And quickly merge themselves in night,
The sharp wind sings its mournful hymn,
    The signs, in heaven and earth, are right;
I heard the wild geese chant their wail,
    From the cold fields of upper air,
Drifting along the northern gale,
    To sunny lakes and islands fair.

The signs are right. The shivering sheep
    Stand huddled by the sheltering wall;
The birds have sought their wintry sleep,
    And lowing cattle wait the stall;

The dead leaves dance their mystic round,
  Whirled by the wind-gusts fierce and wild;
And dry stalks flutter o'er the ground,
  Where late the yellow harvests smiled.

The signs are right. We heard the roar,
  Borne inward from the ocean deeps,
And mad waves broke along the shore,
  And dashed against the rocky steeps:
But household fires burn clear and bright,
  And rest comes after summer toil,
And well-filled garners give delight,
  Treasures of "corn and wine and oil."

It comes, New England's festal day,
  A link in that long golden chain,
Which stretches on its shining way,
  To bring old memories back again;
In all our conflicts and our fears,
  When days were dark, and days were bright,
This day, through our historic years,
  Runs like a magic thread of light.

There rises now before mine eye,
  In pictured beauty soft and clear,
A vision of the days gone by,
  When life was young and joy was near:
A weary tramp among the hills;
  A piercing wind with blinding dust;
A hope that scorned these outer ills,
  And looked beyond in boundless trust;—

THANKSGIVING.

A farm-house with its ponderous frame;
   A grandsire with his silvery hair,
Sitting before the generous flame,
   In his antique and ample chair;
A chimney corner large and warm,
   Where a dear mother sat of old;
Here was a refuge from the storm,
   A shelter from the biting cold.

And all around are signs of cheer,
   Pure incense and an odor sweet,
And kindred hearts are gathered here,
   And joy that comes where kindred meet.
Now let the hovering snow-clouds lower;
   Let winds blow east or winds blow west;
They cannot mar this charmèd hour,
   They cannot hurt this household nest.

Then keep the good old festal day;
   Sing the old songs the fathers sung;
Around your altars kneel to pray;
   Let praises rise from joyful tongue.
God moves in all the rolling year,
   In clouds and tempests, sun and rain;
He bids the tender grass appear,
   And loads the autumn fields with grain.

THE BLACK VALLEY RAILROAD.

You have heard of the ride of John Gilpin,
    That captain so jocund and gay,
How he rode down to Edmonton Village,
    In a very remarkable way.

You have heard of the ride of Mazeppa,
    Bound fast to his wing-footed steed,
How he coursed through the fields and the forests,
    At a very remarkable speed.

But I sing of a trip more exciting,
    In a song which I cannot restrain;
Of a ride down the Black Valley Railroad,
    Of a ride on the Black Valley train.

The setting-out place for the journey
    Is Sippington station, I think,
Where the engines for water take whisky,
    And the people take—something to drink.

From collisions you need fear no danger,
    No trains are ever run back,
They all go one way—to perdition,
    Provided they keep on the track.

THE BLACK VALLEY RAILROAD. 107

By the time we reach Medicine village,
    The passengers find themselves sick;
Have leg-ache, or back-ache, or head-ache,
    Or some ache that strikes to the quick.

We are pious and hold by the Scripture,
    With Paul the Apostle agree
To take "wine" instead of much "water,"
    For our "often infirmity."

In fact, we improve on the reading,
    By just a slight change in the text,
Say "often," where the Scripture says "little,"
    And leave "little" for what may come next.

We break up at Tippleton station,
    To try and get rid of our pain;
At Topersville also we tarry,
    And do the same over again.

Our spirits indeed may be willing,
    But very weak is the flesh;
So, oft as we stop for five minutes,
    We use all the time to refresh.

Now we come to the great central station,
    The last stopping place on the line, [house
Drunkard's Curve—where is kept the chief store-
    Of rum, whisky, brandy and wine.

From this place on to Destruction;
    The train makes no break or delay,
And those who may wish to stop sooner
    Are kindly thrown out by the way.

A full supply of bad whisky
    For our engine is taken in here;
And a queer looking fellow from Hades
    Steps on for our engineer.

From Drunkard's Curve to Destruction,
    The train is simply express,
And will not be slowed or halted
    For any flag of distress.

And so when all things are ready,
    From Drunkard's Curve we set out:
Let me give you some flying glimpses
    Of the places along the route.

First, Rowdyville claims our attention;
    Then Quarrelton comes into view;
Then Riotville breaks on the vision,
    And the filthy Beggartown too.

As we rush by the village of Woeland,
    Three wretches are thrown from the train;
We can see them rolled over and over,
    Through the darkness, the mud and the rain.

Our engineer chuckles and dances
    In the wild lurid flashes he throws;
Hotter blaze the red fires of his furnace,
    As on into blackness he goes.

O the sounds that we hear in the darkness,
    The laughter and crying and groans,
The ravings of anger and madness,
    The sobbings and pitiful moans!

For now we have entered the regions
  Where all things horrible dwell,
Where the shadows are peopled with goblins,
  With the fiends and the furies of hell.

In this deep and stygian darkness,
  Lost spirits have made their abode;
It is plain—we are near to Destruction,
  Very near to the end of the road.

Would you like, my young friends, to take passage
  To this region of horror and pain?
Here stretches the Black Valley Railroad,
  And here stands the Black Valley train.

TIME FOR THANKSGIVING.

When the cold winds out of the north
  With a mournful song go by;
When the forests are leafless and gaunt,
  And the pastures and meadows are dry;
When the wild geese have taken their flight,
  And gone to a sunnier home;
When the day passes quick into night,
  It is time for Thanksgiving to come.

When the pumpkins, and apples, and corn,
  Are all gathered in from the cold;
When the cribs unto bursting are filled,
  With the ripe ears, yellow as gold;

TIME FOR THANKSGIVING.

When the oxen, the cows and the sheep,
   No more on the hillsides must roam;
When it rains, or it hails, or it snows,
   It is time for Thanksgiving to come.

When the hazy, the still, dreamy days
   Of the Indian summer are o'er;
When the squirrels have ransacked the woods,
   And laid up the nuts, in great store;
When the earth is all dreary and waste,
   And the skies look scowling and glum;
When the dead leaves go whirling along,
   It is time for Thanksgiving to come.

When John, who is learning a trade,
   And Julia, away at her school,
And Dick, at his college and books,
   And Jane, at her needle and spool;
With Mary, and Charley and Joe,
   Are all packing off to go home,
Afoot, on the coach, in the cars,
   It is time for Thanksgiving to come.

When in cottage and farm-house afar,
   As gather the shadows of night,
The fires with new energy burn,
   And gleam with a wonderful light;
For they welcome the wanderers back,
   They beckon in many who roam;
Then blest be the day, the joyous day,
   The time for Thanksgiving is come.

MY LITTLE PLAYMATE.

I AM a grandsire, journeying close
    On threescore years and ten;
And when my daily tasks are done,
    And laid aside my pen,
I call my little playmate in
    Now passing on to three,
For I have need as much of her
    As she has need of me.

She draws me from the world of fact,
    With all its selfish strife,
She breaks the prosy lines of thought,
    That make up common life;
She lures me to her little world,
    Where airy creatures dwell.
Where all things dance in joy and light
    Beneath some magic spell.

She wakes again those dreamy songs
    That never yet were sung,
Which thrill through happy little hearts,
    But not through human tongue;
She carols like a morning lark
    To usher in the day,
And bring back memories from a land
    That lieth far away.

MY LITTLE PLAYMATE.

Her roundelays and jingles make
    Such music in my ear,
With all her tricksy words and ways,
    I cannot choose but hear:
We leave all other verse aside,
    For that small classic lore
Which Mother Goose has garnered up
    In her undying store:

The naughty ways of Johnny Greene,
    The virtuous Johnny Stout;
The boy in blue who lay asleep
    When cow and sheep were out;
The robin sitting in the barn,
    With head beneath his wing,
Because the snow is on the ground,
    And he is cold, poor thing;

The accident to Jack and Jill,
    The hurrying little Jane,
The man who scratched out both his eyes,
    And scratched them in again;
The active cow that jumped the moon,
    The bull that tolled the bell,
These are a few,—but many more,
    Too numerous to tell.

And then we play at coop and seek;
    The mystery is small;
We hide behind the nearest chair,
    Or in the open hall;

And every time that search is made
   Within this same small round,
The happy shout of joy goes up
   Because the lost is found.

Oh, let me never grow too old
   To join in merry glee
With any bright and laughing child
   That climbs upon my knee;
Let me still keep the sportive mind
   Until my dying day,
For what is life, in all its length,
   Without the children's play?

A SONG FOR MAY DAY.

"For lo! the winter is past,
   The singing of birds has come;"
Softly, my friend, not quite so fast,
   Stay close by your fire at home.

"Come, let us go forth to the fields,
   For the voice of the turtle is heard;"
I have tried it myself and know what it yields,
   You will wish you never had stirred.

"I know of a beautiful bank,
   Whereon the wild flowers grow;"
Go search for it then, through meadows dank,
   You will find it a bank of snow.

A SONG FOR MAY DAY.

"How sweet is the breath of spring!
  How joyous the coming of May!"
That is the way the poets sing,
  And have for many a day.

I have heard this piping of old,
  And have often been fooled by the tune;
I have caught me many an ugly cold,
  All for not waiting till June.

You cannot render it warm,
  By buying of green-house flowers;
You cannot break an easterly storm,
  By prating of sunny bowers.

So put up your chaplets so gay,
  All made of paper and strings;
And patiently wait for the better day
  Which June in its mildness brings.

Build you a wholesome fire,
  And let the sun into your room;
And read of May to your heart's desire,
  With an air-tight to soften its gloom.

LYRICAL.

FIRST PSALM.
[Closely rendered.]   L. M.

Blest is the man, who walketh not
  Where men of evil counsel meet,
Who stands not in the sinner's way,
  Nor sitteth in the scorner's seat.

But in Jehovah's perfect law
  He ever findeth his delight;
Thereon he meditates by day,
  And meditates thereon by night.

He shall be like some goodly tree,
  Planted where streams of water flow;
Which bringeth forth its timely fruit,
Whose leaf no blasting heat shall know.

His toil, prosperity shall crown;
  While the ungodly toil in vain:
Their work is like the fleeting chaff,
  Which the wind scatters o'er the plain.

So the ungodly shall not stand,
  When judgment comes to try their way;
In the assembly of the just
  The guilty sinner shall not stay.

The Lord keeps watch about the path,
  And knows the way the righteous go;
But the ungodly man shall fail,
  His way shall perish here below.

FOREFATHERS' DAY.

Portuguese Hymn.

O STRONG is our God in the might of his sway,
He speaks, and the seas and the tempests obey;
He guides the frail bark on its perilous path,
And holds back the surges that break in their wrath.

O strong is our God, for He casteth down kings,
But broods o'er the humble with sheltering wings;
He shames and dishonors the pride of the throne,
But lifts up the lowly and makes them His own.

O strong is our God, for this realm of the west
He guarded and kept for a refuge and rest,
He gave to our fathers these fountains and rills,
The wealth of the valleys and strength of the hills.

O strong is our God, and what song shall unfold
The wonders He wrought for our fathers of old?
Through sorrow and gladness, in sunshine and storm,
Their faith still beheld His invisible form.

O strong is our God, and the nations are strong
That bow in His temples with worship and song;
The fear of the Lord is the strength of the State,
And blest are the men at His altars who wait.

HYMN FOR PEACE.
Keller's American Hymn.

CALM on the hills of the east was the night,
　Softly the dew fell on valley and plain,
Bright was the star with its mystical light,
　Through the still air came the angels' refrain,
　Song, which the hills caught and echoed again:
"Glory to God, where He dwells in His height,
　Peace and good will among men shall remain,"
Song of all songs, on that wonderful night.

Earth, thou art weary with tumult and war;
　Armies march o'er thee with desolate tread;
Weeping and moaning are heard from afar,
　Groans from the dying and grief for the dead,
　Households in anguish bemoaning their dead:
Earth, thou art worn with this carnage and jar,
　Why should thine empires sit trembling with dread?
Shake from thy shoulders these burdens of war.

Lo, the day breaks, seen by prophets of old,
　Day, when the noise of the battle shall cease;
Lo, the day dawns by the angels foretold,
　Christ shall be king o'er an empire of peace:
　Nations shall walk in the sunlight of peace:
So shall come on the fair ages of gold,
　So shall the kingdom and glory increase;
Lift then the song of that midnight of old.

SAFETY OF THE STATE.

C. M. Double.

The little springs and sparkling rills
    In lonely places hide;
They run among the ancient hills,
    And through the shadows glide;
Their birth-place is the wilderness;
    From mountain wilds they go,
By many winding paths, to bless
    The thirsty vales below.

God guards these little mountain springs,
    Nor lets their channels dry;
He hovers on his cloudy wings
    From out the stormy sky;
He giveth rain, and snow like wool,
    And feeds this ceaseless flow,
To make the lowlands beautiful,
    And waving harvests grow.

The strength that makes a nation great,
    In secret is supplied;
The energies that build the State,
    In humble virtues hide;
From Christian homes among the hills,
    The streams of influence flow,—
The force that fights with earthly ills,
    And overcomes the foe.

And if these little fountains fail,
    And little streamlets dry,
No art or cunning can avail;
    The nation's self must die:
But if the mountain streams are pure,
    And constant in their flow,
The nation's heritage is sure,
    In all the plains below.

THE GOOD MAN'S DEATH.

L. M.

Go take thy rest: the day is done,
    And all its toil and burden o'er,
No more the heat of burning sun,
    The pelting storm shall break no more.

Go take thy rest: a good man dies,
    And yields his spirit back to God;
But on his path a radiance lies,
    A light o'er all the fields he trod.

Go take thy rest: the night comes on,
    And stars shine out along the sky;
But night foretells a fairer dawn,
    Whene'er the good and faithful die.

DEDICATION OF THE SCHOOL-HOUSE.
America.

This labor of our hands,
Which now in fulness stands,
   To Thee we bring:
God, whom our fathers sought,
Great Source of light and thought,
For Thee our hands have wrought
   This offering.

Not for vain pomp and show,
Did we our care bestow,
   These walls to rear:
But that our sons may rise,
With clear discerning eyes,
And daughters may be wise
   Thy name to fear.

Here lead and guide our youth,
In paths of grace and truth,
   And make them strong;
That they may still abide
Firmly on virtue's side,
Nor turn, in scorn and pride,
   To shame and wrong.

Fixed on this chosen soil,
This crown of all our toil,
　　Long may it stand
In finished strength and grace,
To form our rising race,
To cheer our dwelling-place,
　　And bless our land.

SABBATH-SCHOOL CELEBRATION.
L. M.

Along the track of vanished years,
　Through storm and sunshine, cold and heat,
To-day our fancy wakes and hears
　The happy tread of little feet.

Before us pass the youthful throngs,
　Walking in Zion's quiet ways;
We catch the pleasant Sabbath songs,
　Rising to heaven on wings of praise.

And back, upon our listening ear,
　Comes that low murmur, ever sweet,
When youthful voices, soft and clear,
　The Saviour's blessed words repeat.

In pastures green, by waters still,
　Through fields in living beauty drest,
He takes us up to Zion's hill,
　His home of everlasting rest.

OMNISCIENCE.

Psalm 139.   7s & 6s.

O God, thine eye all-seeing
  Watches and knows my way;
To thee my inmost being
  Stands open day by day;
My sitting, my uprising,
  Are ever in thy sight,
And vain is my disguising
  Beneath the shades of night.

If thy pure precepts scorning,
  I haste afar to flee,
If on the wings of morning
  I seek the utmost sea;
Up to the heavens ascending;
  Hiding in depths below;
Still on my step attending,
  Thou watchest where I go.

From Thee, the all-discerning,
  Where can frail mortals hide?
Where, from Thy presence turning,
  Shall guilty souls abide?
Before me and behind me
  Thy form is ever nigh,
In darkness thou dost find me,
  As in the noon-day sky.

Search me, O God, and know me,
   Try me and know my heart;
My inward evil show me,
   And bid my sin depart;
Still watch and walk beside me,
   Lest from thy truth I stray,
And let thy right hand guide me
   The everlasting way.

OUR NATIVE LAND.

Keller's American Hymn.

LAND of our sires and the hope of the free,
   Land which the God of our fathers hath blest,
On through the ages to come, shalt thou be
   Home, where the exiled and weary find rest:
   Home, where the storm-tost and weary find rest:
Open thy gates to the ships of the sea,
   Beckon the wanderers in to the west,
Open thy gates, O thou land of the free!

God, in the past, has encamped round thy way,
   Guarded thy footsteps with wisdom and might;
Led thee with pillar of cloud through the day,
   Led thee with pillar of fire through the night;
   Kept thee in battle and tempest and night:
Still let the nation acknowledge His sway,
   Still let the people be strong in His might,
God shall encamp round thy dangerous way.

Build thy strong empire from sea unto sea,
    Mountain and valley shall smile in thy light;
Build upon truth this abode of the free,
    Then shall thine empire stand fast in its might,
    Then shall thine empire wax great in its might;
Blazoned on all thy fair banners shall be,
    Liberty, guarded by justice and right:
Stretch then thine empire from sea unto sea.

ZION'S GLORY.

7s & 6s.

Arise and shine in gladness,
    O Zion, loved of old!
Long were thy years of sadness,
    Thy pains and toils untold;
Most wonderful thy story,
    Through all the ages past:
But God will make his glory
    To shine o'er thee at last.

Strong are thy deep foundations,
    Thy walls stand fast in might,
And far off Gentile nations
    Shall call thee their delight.
Thy fame the earth shall cover,
    From east to utmost west,
And round thee tribes shall hover,
    As birds about their nest.

ZION'S GLORY.

All lands shall yield their treasure,
    All islands of the sea,
In full o'erflowing measure,
    And pour it out to thee.
The kings of earth shall bring thee
    Their ancient stores of gold,
And merchant princes fling thee
    The hoarded wealth of old.

Fair Sheba, which entices
    The kingdoms with her stores,
Shall bring her wealth of spices,
    Her gems and costly ores;
And Midian's traffic rangers
    Shall throng thine ample halls;
And far-off sons of strangers
    Shall build thy massive walls.

Zion, the loved, has waited
    In sorrow and in tears,
Forsaken, scorned and hated,
    Through the long weary years.
Now will I put upon her
    A crown of matchless worth,
An make her name an honor,
    A praise in all the earth.

Her sun no more declining,
    Shall shed perpetual light;
Her moon in splendor shining,
    With beauty clothe the night;

Her doors wide open flinging,
  In queenly rest she waits,
While the lost race with singing
  Comes thronging to her gates.

OUR LAND.
10s.

This land, O God, which Thy right hand has kept,
  A large dominion stretching wild and free,
Which through the lonely ages still has slept,
  With all its treasured stores from sea to sea,—

Make it an Empire fit to be thine own,
  Crowned with the glory of the latter days;
Here may Immanuel build His stately throne,
  And fill the sounding forests with His praise.

Not fields, or flocks, or thickly crowded marts,
  Or white-winged ships sailing o'er every sea,—
Not golden ores, or gems, or polished arts,
  Can make a people truly strong and free.

Thy grace alone can lift to high estate
  The lowliest souls which thy pure truth has stirred;
'Tis Thine to make a nation strong and great,
  Reared on the mighty pillars of Thy word.

In human arm we dare not make our boast,
  And not in fruitful acres fair and broad;
Not in the refuge of an arméd host,
  But only in the mighty arm of God.

BAPTISMAL HYMN.

7s Double.

Father, to thy sheltering wing,
This dear child in faith we bring:
Poor and blind and weak are we,
All our help must come from Thee:
At thy footstool would we bow,
While we breathe our humble vow:
Hear, O hear our earnest prayer,
Take this child beneath thy care.

Blessed Jesus, Son of God,
Who these earthly paths hast trod;
Thou did'st call, with accent sweet,
Little children to thy feet:
Let this little child be thine,
Sheltered by thy love divine:
Hear, O hear our earnest prayer,
Take this child beneath thy care.

Holy Spirit, meek and mild,
Shed thy graces on this child;
Let this crystal water be
Emblem meet of purity;
Make the spirit white and clean,
Cleanse the soul from sense and sin:
Hear, O hear our earnest prayer,
Take this child beneath thy care.

THE ANCIENT SABBATH SCHOOL.
H. M.

In memory's golden light,
   How pure the past appears!
How calmly on the sight
   Rise the long vanished years!
With joy we tell the story o'er,
Of days that shall return no more.

Again the Sabbath bell
   Rings out its call to prayer,
We hear the music swell
   On the still morning air;
And scattered dwellers far around
Rise and obey that welcome sound.

We see the happy throngs,
   Walking in Zion's ways,
We hear the child-like songs,
   Upborne on wings of praise;
And mingling voices, soft and sweet,
The Saviour's blessed word repeat.

We gather here to-day,
   A broken, way-worn band;
Some are far, far away,
   Some in the better land;
But still our fathers' God we bless,
And sing His love and faithfulness.

Thy word, O God, shall live,
   Though men and nations die;
Thy word its light shall give,
   As years go rolling by;
Roll on, ye years, and bring the hour
When all the earth shall feel its power.

DEDICATION OF HITCHCOCK LIBRARY.

Dec. 21, 1874.

I.   L. M.

God of our Pilgrim sires, to Thee
   All might and majesty belong;
Before Thy face we bow the knee,
   And lift aloud our grateful song.

By Thy strong arm, the Pilgrim band
   Were kept in all their stormy way,
Until they trod this goodly land,
   And gave to us this happy day.

We bring our gift before Thy throne,
   This labor which our hands have wrought,
And consecrate to Thee alone
   This treasure-house of sacred thought.

Choicer than gold, though thrice refined,
   Or all the gems that ocean rolls,
Are these fair riches of the mind,
   This garnered wealth of holy souls.

God of our sires, still let that grace,
   That strength, which made the fathers bold,
Descend upon the Pilgrim race,
   As coming years shall be unrolled.

II.   C. M.

WE sing our gladsome hymn of praise,
   And bless our Fathers' God,
While we recount the former days,
   And trace the pathway trod.

How many hearts this hope has filled,
   The living and the dead!
How many hands have wrought to build
   This temple where we tread!

But one, our warmest praise demands,
   His gift we here recall,
By whom this finished structure stands,
   Whose name adorns our Hall.

He gave, and passed from earth away,
   To his unseen employ,
Ere he could see this crowning day,
   Or share our festive joy.

But here, embalmed, his gift shall last,
   His substance shall endure;
And as the rolling years go past,
   His heritage is sure.

HOME MISSIONS.
7s & 6s.

"The voice of one crying in the wilderness."

A SOUND of glad thanksgiving
   In border lands is heard;
The lonely vales are ringing,
   The forest depths are stirred;
In many a humble dwelling
   By wood and mountain glen,
The messengers are telling
   Of God's great love to men.

O ye who walk in gladness,
   Where God's fair temples rise,
Think of the gloom and sadness
   Beneath those forest skies;
Where sinful souls are turning,
   Bewildered and unblest;
And Christian hearts are yearning
   For the old Sabbath rest.

Ye know the consolation
   Of the sweet word of God,
In days of tribulation,
   When falls the chastening rod;
Go help the sad and weary
   To find this cheering ray,
When clouds hang dark and dreary
   Around their earthly way.

SONG FOR FREEDOM.—NOV. 3, 1868.

Crambambuli.

All hail to the land
  In majesty arising,
From sea to sea, to make men free,
  All hail to the land!
Above the scattering clouds of war
She shines like some bright morning star
O'er nations near and far,
  Hail, hail to the land!

Oh, long was the night
  And fearful was the conflict,
When myriad hosts along our coasts
  Pressed on to the fight.
They trod their grim and bloody way
To give our freedom mightier sway
And bring in a golden day
  For God and the right!

Our brave leader, hail,
  Who bore our armies onward;
Whose gallant form rode out the storm,
  Our brave leader, hail!
To-day the happy millions wait
To bear him on to halls of State,
High amid the good and great,
  Our brave leader, hail!

Then joy to the land
   In majesty arising,
From sea to sea, to make men free,
   Joy, joy to the land!
She shines as shines the morning star
Above the vanished clouds of war,
O'er seas and tribes afar,
   Joy, joy to the land!

OUR FATHERS.

H. M.

WE own that guiding Hand,
   Which, in the years of old,
Led to this chosen land
   Our fathers, firm and bold;
Brought them across the stormy sea,
To build this empire of the free.

They came with faith in God;
   They came with faith in man;
On this fresh virgin sod
   To try their untried plan;
To give this realm of freedom birth,
And shed new light around the earth.

Soon as our godly sires
   These new-found shores had trod,
They lit their altar-fires
   And claimed the land for God;
They filled the forest shades with light,
And turned to day the savage night.

PSALM viii.

10s.

O LORD, our Lord, how excellent Thy name,
Through the wide circuit of this earthly frame!
Above the heavens Thy glorious acts are known,
Far as the habitation of Thy throne.

When I survey the wonders of Thine hand,
The moon and stars that shine at Thy command,
Lord, what is man, Thy creature here below,
The son of man, that Thou should'st love him so?

A little lower than the angels made,
Glory and honor on his head are laid;
For Thou hast given him a kingly seat,
And put all earthly things beneath his feet.

The roving beasts, the cattle of the stall,
The bleating flocks, come trooping at his call;
The birds that fly, the fish that range the sea,
Are made submissive to his high decree.

O Lord, our Lord, how excellent Thy name!
In heaven and earth Thy glory is the same:
Through the far skies Thy mighty acts are known,
Far as the habitation of Thy throne.

INSTALLATION AT OLD SOUTH CHURCH, BOSTON.

Portuguese Hymn.

O God, unto Thee would we gratefully raise
Our songs of remembrance, our anthems of praise;
Enthroned in the heavens, Thou dost stoop to bestow
Thy kindness and care on Thy children below.

Our fathers of old, with a joyful accord,
Inspired by Thy word built an house for the Lord;
They wrought in their weakness, but Thou in Thy might
Hast brought forth their work into fullness of light.

To-day, the far years rise again to our view;
We see the long lines of the faithful and true;
With songs of rejoicing they gladden their way,
Though bearing the burden and heat of the day.

As wave follows wave on the sea-beaten shore,
The pilgrims pass on and earth sees them no more;
Thy years never fail, and the Church of Thy care
From age unto age shall Thy glory declare.

To-day, a new scene opens out on our sight;
Shed round it, O God, the soft beams of Thy light;
While here in Thy courts as Thy people shall bend,
Let power from on high in its fullness descend.

JOB iv. 12–17.

S. M.

A WONDROUS thing was brought,
  In secret, to mine ear;
It stirred to life my slumbering thought,
  And filled my soul with fear.

In visions of the night,
  When deep sleep falls on men,
A spirit passed before my sight,
  And made my boasting vain.

It stood before my face,
  The form I could not see,
But from some shadowy hiding-place,
  A voice spake unto me:

Shall mortal man aspire
  To be more just than God?
Or shall he dream in wild desire
  To fly the chastening rod?

If angels great in might,
  Who circle round the throne,
Are counted simple in his sight,
  And all their folly own;

How shall frail dying man,
  Whose house is in the dust,
Dare to rebuke his Maker's plan,
  Or count His ways unjust!

SONG OF THE REDEEMED.

Revelation xv.   7s & 6s.

They sang the song of Moses,
    The servant of the Lord,
And of the Lamb, once dying,
    But now in heaven adored;
Thus ran the mighty anthem,
    Which angels joined to sing,
Bearing immortal honors
    To Christ their glorious King.

How marvellous Thy workings,
    O Thou Almighty One!
How true and just and righteous,
    The wonders Thou hast done!
Thou King of saints in glory,
    Who shall not fear Thy name?
For Thou most high and holy
    Hast borne the sinner's shame.

Earth's gathering tribes and nations
    Shall round Thy banners come,
Shall flock to pay their worship,
    As exiles hastening home:
For now Thy works of judgment,
    Thy ways of truth and grace,
Are manifest and open
    To Adam's wandering race.

EASTER HYMNS.

I.

BREAK o'er the earth, thou glad prophetic morning,
    For life immortal dawns beneath thy light;
Strong was the grave, and death was full of terror,
    But death lies vanquished by His kingly might.
His tomb is open—see the grave-clothes lying,
    Come see the napkin that was round His head;
Stoop down and wonder, for the dead has vanished—
    At early dawn He left His gloomy bed.

And ye poor mourners who have laid your loved ones,
    With bleeding hearts, in their cold graves to sleep,
And while the storms of earth are sighing round them,
    To your lone chambers have returned to weep—
Our Lord has risen; calm away your sorrow,
    And take the blessed peace that word imparts;
With this sweet comfort, comfort one another,
    And roll the burden from your weary hearts.

Our Lord has risen,—and the word goes sounding,
    In broader circles, o'er the troubled race;
It lifts the lowly, sets the poor and humble,
    The meek and gentle, in a lordly place:
It throws o'er man a calm and heavenly glory,
    And makes the earth companion of the skies;
The dead are waiting for his reappearing,
    And they that sleep in Him, with Him shall rise.

II.

Dark is the grave in which Jesus lies sleeping,
   Heavy the night that encircles His tomb:
They who have loved Him in anguish are weeping,
   All their fair visions are shrouded in gloom.

Out from these shadows, in glory uprising,
   Breaks, in its brightness, the glad Easter morn,
Mountain and valley with splendor baptizing:
   Lo, a new hope for the race has been born.

Christ has arisen,—the seals have been broken,
   Watchmen have kept their night-vigils in vain:
So is fulfilled what the prophets have spoken,
   He who was dead is now living again.

Christ has arisen,—the grave could not hold Him,
   Messengers hasten to tell the surprise;
Angels shall come in their arms to enfold Him,
   Bearing Him up to His throne in the skies.

III.

7s Double.

Hail the bright and radiant morn,
Out of gloom and darkness born!
See, the stone is rolled away
Where the buried Saviour lay!
Let your songs of gladness rise
In full chorus to the skies,
For the long dark night is past,
Life immortal breaks at last.

Now while morning shadows fall,
And earth's happy voices call,
Hasten at the break of day,
Come and see where Jesus lay;
Stoop thee down with wondering eyes,
Fill thy soul with sweet surprise;
Then in joy lift up thy head,
For He liveth who was dead.

Yea, He lives for evermore
On the fair eternal shore,
And His faithful ones who sleep,
He with tenderest care will keep
Till the last great morn shall break,
And His loved ones shall awake:
With the hope this word imparts,
Comfort one-another's hearts.

IV.

Lord, I believe; help thou mine unbelief;
   Teach my dull soul, from earthly thoughts awaking,
To rise o'er doubt, and fear, and present grief,
   For, lo! again the Easter morn is breaking.
From land to land the gladsome tidings run,
   And Easter bells, afar and near, are ringing;
From dawn of morn to set of evening sun,
   The air shall thrill with notes of joy and singing.

There is for man no glory on the earth,
   If the strong gates of death have not been broken:
If we awake not to immortal birth
   By that great word which Christ the Lord has spoken,

Vain are all pomps and shows of earthly life,
  Vain this long round of sorrow and of sinning:
In all the prizes of this selfish strife,
  There is no prize worthy the cost of winning.

Let not your heart be troubled; I am He
  Who once was dead, but now alive forever;
And those who in the dust shall sleep with me
  No art or power from my embrace can sever.
Many the mansions in my Father's home,
  Many the happy dwellers there abiding;
I will prepare a place for you, and come
  To this eternal home your footsteps guiding.

O words of greatness and triumphant power,
  From age to age and land to land resounding!
No words like these in nature's dying hour,
  With strength and lofty hope for man abounding:
When earthly sights and sounds can please no more,
  And in the sleep of death my eyes are closing,
Let me, by faith, behold th' eternal shore,
  On these strong words of Christ, my Lord, reposing.

V.

THE JOURNEY TO EMMAUS.

The tumult and noise of the city
  No longer could trouble their ear,
Yet they toiled o'er the hills on their journey,
  In silence and sadness and fear:

For the thoughts of their hearts were kept busy
    Over one they had loved, who was dead;
The dreams they had dreamed had all vanished,
    And the hopes they had cherished were fled.

The fields far around them were lonely,
    Yet they saw a kind stranger draw near,
Who was touched with the look of their sadness,
    And asked of their trouble and fear;
And they told him of one they had trusted
    As Prince, and Redeemer, and Friend,
But the grave had now claimed him as victim,
    And brought their glad hopes to an end.

Then he opened unto them the Scriptures,
    And made it all plain to their sight,
That the cross and the grave were the pathways
    That led to His kingdom of light;
At the evening repast in their dwelling,
    He was known in the breaking of bread;
And he vanished,—but ere He departed
    They had seen the dear Friend that was dead.

And with joy they said one to the other,
    Were not our hearts burning within,
At his accents so gentle and loving,
    O'erlooking our blindness and sin?
The tomb where he lay could not hold him,
    So he conquered the last of his foes
When the sepulchre bars had been broken,
    And from its cold grave he arose.

CHRISTMAS CAROLS.
7s Double.

I.

Night, with holy silence, fills
Judah's ancient vales and hills,
And the moonlight beauty sleeps
Round her rough and rocky steeps;
While aloft, in heavenly space,
Lo that wondrous star of grace,
Shining down with tranquil ray,
Over where the young child lay.

Wise men, from the lands afar,
Long have watched that moving star;
Night by night, with eager eyes
Tracked its course along the skies,
Till their way-worn feet were led
Safely to the cradle-bed;
Glad to pour the gifts they bring
Down before the new-born king.

It is meet to bring your gold,
And your wealth of myrrh unfold;
He, whom kings and prophets saw,
Comes to magnify the law;
He, the meek and kingly child,
Holy, harmless, undefiled,
Rises from this lowly birth,
Prince of Peace—to rule the earth.

Open thou, O God, mine eyes,
Make them quick to read the skies;
Let no cloud my vision mar,
While I follow Bethlehem's Star;
Lead me like those men of old,
Through the night paths, lone and cold,
Till the star the secret tells
Where my king Immanuel dwells.

II.

O NIGHT of nights! crown of the gathered ages,
    The mighty dream of long prophetic years!
The hoary seers, the ancient saints and sages,
    Watched for thy coming through their patient tears.

O holy night! celestial bells are ringing,
    And heaven bends down the waiting earth to greet:
From airy heights the angel bands are singing,
    And Bethlehem's hills the echoing strains repeat.

O silent night! the quiet dews are falling,
    And moonlight broods o'er vale and mountain steep,
The wakeful shepherds, each to other calling,
    Guard through the midnight hours the gentle sheep.

O wondrous night! yon moving star is tracing
    Its lordly pathway through the Eastern skies:
And now it stands, with heavenly splendor, gracing
    The humble dwelling where the young child lies.

O night of joy! the years to come shall brighten
    Beneath the hallowed light of Bethlehem's star:
A Prince is born, whose gentle sway shall lighten
    The burdened race, and still the noise of war.

THE NEW SETTLEMENTS.

"The desert shall rejoice."   7s Double.

Westward still the pilgrims go,
   Nearer to the setting sun,
On through storm, and heat, and snow,
   Till their mighty task be done;
Bold heroic sons of toil,
   Still they leave the ancient nest,
To subdue the forest soil,
   And to give their children rest.

Let the sower follow fast,
   Laden with the precious grain;
Let the heavenly stores be cast
   Wide o'er hill, and vale, and plain:
God will guard the fruitful seed,
   Will not let this labor die;
For immortal souls must feed
   On the bread of His supply.

In the morning sow thy seed,
   Nor at evening stay thy toil;
Hear how kindred voices plead,
   From that far-off forest soil:
So the wilderness shall bloom,
   In its heavenly beauty clad;
So the deserts lose their gloom,
   And the lonely place be glad.

GOD IN THE GARDEN.

"And they heard the voice of the Lord God walking in the garden in the cool of the day."

AND still God walks upon the earth,
   And talks with men below,
Along the leafy garden paths
   His footsteps come and go;
And when the soul is calm and pure,
   And passion's waves are still,
How sweetly comes that winning voice,
   The listening ear to fill!

O happy is that trustful child,
   Who runs with ready feet,
Along the pleasant garden ways,
   His Father's voice to greet;
But when the soul is full of shame,
   And full of sin and pride,
He runs, as Adam did before,
   Among the trees to hide.

For heaven lies very near to earth,
   And God dwells not apart,
And we shall find Him, when we seek
   With purity of heart;
We hear Him walking mid the trees,
   Wherever we may stray,
He meets us in the garden paths,
   At the cool close of day.

YALE SONGS.

Sung at different Yale Alumni meetings in Boston.

Crambambuli.

I.

1 Oh, gladly to-night,
As children of one household,
We grasp the hand, a joyous band,
In gladness to-night;
We drive our carking cares away,
And give our memories leave to play
Around youth's golden day,
That day ever bright.

Oh, sweet day of youth!
When every pulse was bounding,
When joys were long, and hopes were strong,
Oh, sweet day of youth!
We catch thy music from afar,
Thy light is like some radiant star,
No mists and clouds to mar,
Serene, pure as truth.

But tears for the dead!
Cut off in life's bright morning,
Companions dear, no longer here,
Tears, tears for the dead!

With them we walked in sweet delight,
With them we climbed the mountain height,
  Oh, were they here to-night
    With light on their head!

    Our good Mother dear,
When she counts up her offspring,
May proudly boast a mighty host
    Of sons far and near;
And in whatever climes they dwell,
They treasure up her counsels well,
  All her kind ways they tell—
    Yea *kind*, when severe.

    Far, far o'er the earth,
Her sons to-night are scattered;
In western lands, on Afric sands,
    Far, far o'er the earth.
They teach the truths their mother taught,
They work the work at which she wrought,
  Their toil with pleasure fraught,
    To show forth her worth.

    Then gladly to-night,
As children of one household,
We grasp the hand, a joyous band,
    In gladness to-night;
We drive our carking cares away,
And give our memories leave to play
  Around youth's golden day,
    That day ever bright.

II.
The Old Mountain Tree.

We are children all of a common home,
   Of a common mother dear,
From the east and west to-night we have come,
   And we gather in gladness here;
We remember yet and can never forget,
   When we sat by our good mother's knee,
When she taught us to walk and taught us to talk,
   And to try how good we could be,
   And to try how good we could be.

We are older grown and are scattered wide,
   But gladly we come once more,
And in thought go back to our mother's side,
   To our home by the sunny shore;
To the pleasant shade where oft we strayed,
   In our converse glad and free,
To the rocky height which day and night
   Stands sentinel guard by the sea,
   Stands sentinel guard by the sea.

Those days of our youth can never come back,
   They have gone like a dream of the night,
But memory wanders along their track,
   With ever-increasing delight;
We tell them o'er, those pleasures of yore,
   And they never can wearisome be,
And we drop a tear for the friends so dear,
   Whose faces no longer we see,
   Whose faces no longer we see.

III.

Evening Bells.

Those days of old, those days of old,
Gone fleeting like a tale long told:
A dimness gathers o'er the eye,
And thoughts go trooping swiftly by,
As backward come to us once more
The memories of those days of yore.

Oh days of youth, when hope was strong
And life was like a pleasant song,
When hand in hand we wandered free,
And talked of all we hoped to be,
With skies above us shining bright,
And earth bedecked with golden light!

How fair before our eager eyes,
Did all the unknown future rise!
But many a heart, then young and brave,
Now slumbers in the silent grave,
And hears no more the story told,
The memory of those days of old.

Those days of old, those days of old,
No more for us can be unrolled;
But as we run our earthly race,
And age comes on with creeping pace,
Our faith would grasp the things before,
And calmly view th' eternal shore.

IV.
Sparkling and Bright.

SING we in praise of the olden days,
    When the pulse of youth was bounding,
When the earth was bright with a charméd light,
    And the songs of joy were sounding;

    Then let us sing, till the arches ring,
        Of the happy years gone o'er us,
    And tell the tale of our life at YALE,
        Till the visions rise before us.

O the years of life, they are vexed with strife,
    And full of pain and sorrow,
And the loads we bear, of toil and care,
    Will press again to-morrow;

    Then let us sing, &c.

We will walk once more on the moonlit shore,
    With the starry heavens above us,
Or sit and dream by the rippling stream
    Of the bright-eyed girls that love us.

    Then rise and sing, &c.

Now here we stand, and give our hand,
    As brother pledges brother;
That come what may, we must still obey
    Our good old Christian Mother.

    Then rise and sing, &c.

THE STILL SMALL VOICE.
C. M. Double.

Amid the noisy whirl of life,
    Its tumult and its fear,
There is a soft and winning voice,
    Comes whispering in my ear;
I hear it in the busy day,
    In stillness of the night,
And though I flee, it follows me,
    In darkness and in light.

The thunder hath a mighty tongue,
    The earthquake speaks in wrath,
And howling winds declare God's will,
    Along their stormy path;
But mightier than the tempest's breath,
    Or thunder rolling loud,
Is that soft word, in stillness heard,
    Where stoutest hearts are bowed.

On land or sea, in storm or calm,
    This still small voice is nigh;
But when I hear God's holy word,
    It speaks most tenderly;
It tells me of my sin and guilt,
    It tells of God's great love;
To hide my shame, it names that Name,
    All other names above.

THE TORN BATTLE-FLAGS.
7s & 6s.

On Forefathers' Day, 1865, the battle flags which had been carried through the war of the Rebellion by the Massachusetts Regiments, were taken from the State House, where they were deposited, and once more carried by the remnants of those regiments through the streets of Boston, in a long and impressive procession.

HAIL to the proud old banner!
Through storm and tempest borne,
Stript of its early splendors,
In conflict scarred and torn:
Its wavy folds have fluttered
In the hot battle's breath,
Its stars have shone triumphant,
On the red field of death.

Hail to its brave defenders!
The glorious boys in blue,
Who, for their God and country,
Have fought the battle through:
Let men and maidens gather
Their glad return to meet,
And let the loud huzzas ring out,
Along the crowded street.

This day is for the Fathers,
Those brave old Pilgrim Sires,

Who kindled in these forests
  The light of Freedom's fires:
These fires are watched and tended,
  By those who bear their name,
And many a son has fallen
  To guard the sacred flame.

Then hail to the proud old banner!
  Through storm and tempest borne,
Stript of its early splendors,
  In conflict scarred and torn:
Its wavy folds have fluttered
  In the hot battle's breath,
Its stars have shone triumphant,
  On the red field of death.

HYMNS FOR FREEDOM.

I.

THE place we tread is holy ground,
  Since that far April morn,
When out of storm and battle sound,
  A mighty hope was born.

We wander o'er these ancient ways,
  And trace the bloody track;
Once more the old heroic days
  In happy thoughts come back.

And unto God we lift our song,
  Who made our fathers bold,
Bore up their hearts with courage strong
  Through those dark days of old.

And by His work in them inwrought,
  He gave fair freedom sway,
Till a great people now is brought
  To keep its festal day.

II.

We lift our glad adoring songs,
  Almighty God, to Thee:
For to Thyself the power belongs
  To make a nation free.

O'er all the earth, from age to age,
  The tribes, that knew not God,
Have bowed beneath the tyrant's rage,
  And felt his scourging rod.

But where Thy Holy Word has shed
  O'er human souls its light,
There nations rise as from the dead,
  And stand in freedom's might.

So would we come, on bended knee,
  Thy mind and will to read,
For when Thy Word has made us free,
  We shall be free indeed.

NOCTURN.

L. M.

Come, with thy shadows, gentle night,
    And fold us in thy blissful calm;
Our eyes grow weary with the light,
    Shed o'er them thy refreshing balm.

From hill and dale, from wood and plain,
    Thy pensive music, soft and low,
Steals on the ear, a sweet refrain,
    How soothing in its murmurous flow!

Come cloudless night!—unbar the gates
    That hide the wonders of the skies;
Unlock the starry realm, that waits
    To gleam on our uplifted eyes.

For noise and tumult fill the day
    In all our busy rounds of care;
Now let the spirit soar away,
    And wander in these fields of air.

Come holy night!—we walk alone,
    And wisdom whispers in our ear;
How winning in her heavenly tone,
    How blest the soul that bends to hear!

JUBILATE DEO.
Ps. 95. 8s.

O come let us sing to the Lord,
   And lift up our voice in His praise,
Come join with a gladsome accord,
   To worship the Ancient of Days.
With anthems encircle His throne,
   With lofty and jubilant songs,
For He is Jehovah alone,
   To Him the dominion belongs.

He fashioned the depths of the earth,
   The hills are the work of His hand,
He gave to the ocean its birth,
   He measured and moulded the land.

O come to our Maker and Head,
   And bow at His altars in prayer,
For us His fair pastures are spread,
   And we are the sheep of His care.

CENTENNIAL CELEBRATION OF TOLLAND COUNTY, AT TOLLAND, CONNECTICUT.

July 4, 1876.

On these ancient hills we gather,
    Now in summer glory dressed;
We have come to tread the pathways
    Which our fathers' feet have pressed:
Lo, the century fills its cycle
    Since our nation's wondrous birth,
And the broad land stirs with gladness,
    Wakes with song and festal mirth.

God's great works are still abiding;
    Changing seasons come and go;
Summer brings her tropic splendors;
    Winter wraps the earth in snow;
On these green and rocky pastures
    Softly yet the dew distils;
Brooks, along their winding channels,
    Still go singing down the hills.

Night lights up the heavenly archway
    With the flaming lamps of old;
Bold Orion treads his circuit,
    In his belt of shining gold;

CELEBRATION AT TOLLAND. 159

Still Arcturus keeps his night-watch,
    Round about the icy north,
And the star of love, at evening,
    With the twilight shade peeps forth.

But frail man, though high and godlike,
    Bears the stamp of mortal birth;
Full of thoughts and glorious visions,
    For a while he treads the earth;
Then to God, who gave him being,
    He restores th' immortal trust,
And is gathered to his fathers,
    Sleeping with his kindred dust.

Round us now the dead are thronging,
    Those heroic men of toil,
Who subdued these rocky hillsides,
    Broke this hard and stubborn soil;
Men who dared defy a tyrant,
    Dared to face a monarch's frown,
Spurned the pride and pomp of kingcraft,
    Spurned the bauble of a crown.

Let us catch some open vision
    Of that world wherein they dwelt;
Of their lonely scattered dwellings,
    Of the altars where they knelt:
Winter firesides large and ample,
    Chimney corners snug and warm,
Coverts from the windy tempest,
    Shelters from the angry storm.

CELEBRATION AT TOLLAND.

Meeting-houses, square and sturdy,
  Ancient temples of renown,
Built near heaven, and glorifying
  Highest points in all the town;
Like the tribes that climbed Mount Zion,
  So our fathers had a way,
Going up to reach their temples,
  Up to keep their festal day.

And the ancient towns were planted
  Up where God's free breezes blow;
While deep solitude and silence
  Reigned in woody vales below;
Then the gods that rule the valleys
  Had not waked the clattering mills:
Then New England's pride and glory
  Were the farms among the hills.

Let us walk these ancient ranges,
  Look about with reverent eyes,
Count the goodly towers and bulwarks
  In their order as they rise;
Let us trace the olden townships,
  Builded in a stately row,
See the world our fathers lived in
  Back one hundred years ago.

———

We start upon the upward line,
  And slowly travel down:
There's little Union, tough and brave,
  The northeast corner town;

CELEBRATION AT TOLLAND.

No town more freely sent her sons
    To that old bloody fray;
And little Union kindly gives
    Our Orator to-day.*

And next comes Stafford, with her Springs,
    Perennial in their flow,
Which cured all sorts of invalids
    A hundred years ago:
The Saratoga of its time,
    Bethesda of its day,
Where fashion gathered with disease,
    And went in health away.

The same old story then as now;
    To sick and halt and lame,
If angels only stirred the pool,
    The blessings surely came;
While Dr. Willard, on the hill,
    Whose christian name was John,
For fifty years proclaimed the word,
    And held securely on.

And Somers had her Doctor too,
    A famous man of yore,
Who taught young scribes divinity,
    And other kindred lore;
For Dr. Backus was the man,
    Commissioned by the state,
To teach her theologues to think,
    And likewise to orate.

* Rev. Charles Hammond, LL.D., for thirty years and more principal of Monson Academy. Born in Union, Conn., June 15, 1813.

CELEBRATION AT TOLLAND.

Fair Ellington, that goodly town,
    Was but a parish then;
But she could show her muster-roll
    Of brave and sturdy men;
And Willington, with pastures rough,
    And here and there a rock,
With Noble for her minister,
    Sent forth her warlike stock.

But for a steady ministry,
    A long enduring calm,
Unchanging through those troubled years,
    Old Tolland bears the palm:
Good Dr. Nathan Williams stretched
    His ministerial line,
From seventeen hundred sixty,
    To eighteen twenty-nine.

And did you ever climb on foot
    To where old Bolton stands?
And did you ever look about
    And wish you owned those lands?
But Bolton was a famous town,
    Back in the olden time,
And kept a famous minister,
    With her own name to rhyme.

She sought for the proprieties,
    The fitnesses of things;
She helped young poets to aspire,
    And use their budding wings;.

And so for half a century,
  Bolton sat still and heard,
While Parson Colton, tall and quaint,
  Proclaimed to them the word.

But Bolton had a pleasant farm,
  A neat and trim estate,
Just northward from her hills of rock,
  And beds of mica slate,
Just where the sharp and shaggy cliffs
  Melt into sandstone soil,
And where the landscape's wavy lines
  In graceful circles coil.

There classic Tankeroosan ran,
  Fed by the mountain rills;
And there the foaming Hockanum
  Went leaping down the hills;
And there good parson Kellogg preached,
  And passed his life away,
And left his lineage behind,
  An honored name to-day.

The Vernon folks, they used to say,
  Were just a little proud;
They held their heads a trifle high,
  Because they were allowed
To leave the ancient granite hills,
  And bring their substance down,
And have a parish by themselves,
  Which grew to be a town.

[The speaker pauses here to state,
    That in his humble way,
He helped to raise the meeting-house
    Which Vernon has to-day:
He helped, by sipping of the punch,
    Which flowed in large supplies,
By tossing pins for men to catch,
    And eating of the pies.]

Old Mansfield sends her honored names
    Along from age to age,
And Dr. Richard Salter lives
    On many a glowing page:
Her scholars and her men of war
    Have earned a just renown,
And send their gathered laurels back,
    To dignify the town.

We tarry next at Coventry,
    At parish number one,
Where Stephen Burroughs went to school
    To parson Huntington;
And then we pass to number two,
    Where Rev. Nathan Strong
Filled out his earthly ministry,
    Full half a century long.

Upon this consecrated soil,
    Brave Nathan Hale was born;
Whose noble deeds and burning words
    Th' historic page adorn.

O, fearful was that stern decree,
  And bloody the command,
That doomed this patriot youth to die,
  A martyr for his land.

For life was sweet and hope was strong,
  And love, with rainbow light,
Made all the future prospects gleam
  In beauty on his sight;
Calmly he saw that light depart,
  And death shades drawing nigh,
He died for his beloved land,
  As only heroes die.

Over that martyr grave we drop
  Our tender tears to-day,
For names like his forever live,
  And cannot pass away.
Long as our liberties shall last,
  And virtue shall prevail,
Our unborn sons will safely keep
  The name of NATHAN HALE.

And next, Columbia as of old
  Sits silent on her hills,
But she has sent her influence forth
  In many widening rills;
For Dr. Wheelock did not take
  Her glory all away,
When he removed that Indian school *
  Up where the forests lay.

* Moor's Indian Charity School, which Dr. Eleazer Wheelock took up to Hanover, N. H., and which soon became Dartmouth College.

We count the names upon her roll,
    And tell her glories o'er,
How she sent out her college boys
    In numbers by the score;
And many an honored name is traced
    Back to her rocky height,
Which, in the after years, became
    A bright and shining light.

And so Columbia touched the world
    Alike through church and state;
Her parson Brockway had a son
    Whose name was Diodate;
He served the church in Ellington,
    While fifty years rolled on,
And furnished for the County's use
    A man, whose name was John.*

So reach we now the peaceful vale,
    Where old Hop river flows,
Winding along its verdant banks,
    And singing as it goes.
Not the fair vale of Rasselas,
    That home of ancient bliss,
Which slept amid the circling hills,
    Had greater charms than this.

How often in the days of youth,
    When hope was clear and bright,
I've journeyed through that pleasant dale
    By dwellings clean and white;

---

* Hon. John H. Brockway, a most useful public man, and M. C. 1839—1843.

I've seen the valley, when it felt
  The rosy breath of June,—
I've seen it, when its meadows slept
  Beneath the harvest moon.

And when the iron horse was sent
  Along this grassy way,
To break the ancient quietude
  With his infernal neigh,
He seemed some dragon, gaily dressed,
  Some demon in disguise,
Like Satan, when, in friendly garb,
  He entered Paradise.

And this sweet vale of Andover
  Saw a fair child arise,
Who now has closed his earthly toil,
  And passed within the skies;
His graceful labors stand impressed
  On many a learned page,
And Dr. Sprague's most noble name *
  Shall live from age to age.

So now we bid the vale adieu,
  And mount to Gilead's height,—
From Gilead's rocks the prophet came,
  Elijah the Tishbite;
To keep the ancient record good,
  Elijah reappears,
To fill old Gilead's ministry,
  For five and forty years.

* Rev. William B. Sprague, D.D., of Albany, author of Annals of the American Pulpit, 9 vols., and many other works.

There was a Lothrop to his name;
  And, as the story goes,
He saw, one Sabbath afternoon,
  His hearers in repose;
He stopped and said—"Of all my flock,
  One half are fast asleep,
And it seems pitiful enough
  To make the angels weep."

Up sprang a bold parishioner,
  Whose righteous soul was stirred,
And looking round, said he "Not quite,
  I think about a third."
By this the sleepers were awake,
  For the remaining way,
And heard what earnest closing words
  The preacher had to say.

At last we enter Hebron town,
  Place of ancestral rest,
Where our brave patriot fathers caught
  A Tory in the nest.
I heard the story in my youth,
  The strange exciting tale,
How nearly Parson Peters * came
  To riding on a rail.

I heard it from the lips of one
  Who saw that cavalcade:
The fiery horsemen from the towns,
  On their tumultuous raid;

---

* Rev. Samuel A. Peters, D.D., LL.D., an Episcopal minister, author of an imaginary history of Connecticut.

And Parson Peters sought a home
    Beyond the briny sea,
And there he nourished his revenge
    And wrote his history.

Hence came that famous code of "Laws,"
    Denominated "Blue,"
Which though a thousand times denied,
    Will still turn up as true;
Do what we will, we cannot hope
    That ancient lie to stay,
And see it fairly laid to rest,
    Until the Judgment day.

In closing this survey, we wish
    To recapitulate,
And if our metre will allow,
    A marvellous fact to state:
There were, one hundred years ago,
    As we have made our rounds,
Just sixteen parishes within
    These ancient county bounds.

Each parish had its minister,
    A man of college lore,
Whose average ministry held on
    To forty years and more;
Is it not healthy to review
    This ancient land of rocks,
Where pastors stayed till hair grew gray,
    And slept amid their flocks?

Let us return once more along our track,
And bring an old and simple legend back:
A tale of truth, and yet a tale untold,
A homely record from those days of old.
A stout young farmer on the Hebron soil,
Just come of age, with ready hands for toil,
Had settled down for his laborious life,
With rocky farm, with young industrious wife,
When the wild sounds from Lexington were heard,
And the new household with the cry was stirred;
But through the scenes of seventeen seventy-five,
He stayed at home to guard the forming hive.
In seventy-six the war cloud rolled away
And settled grimly round Manhattan Bay;
Ere spring had passed, that ringing call for men
Went through our little State from hill to glen:
Old Put had sounded out the bold refrain,
And Trumbull called, who never called in vain.
So the young farmer hastened to the strife;
Left the spring work, and left his faithful wife,
Kissed the young babe, their first and new-born child,
Soothed the young mother with his accents mild,
Shouldered his gun and vanished o'er the hill,
To join the camp, and learn a soldier's drill.
He counted that the rules of war would yield,
Ere his departure to the distant field,
A respite brief, a passing day's reprieve
To come once more and take his parting leave.
But in this camp life, short had been his stay,
When came a summons brooking no delay.
The troops must hasten to the scene of strife;
He penned a hasty message to his wife,

To send the garments, which her hands had wrought,
Those products of her lonely silent thought.
But the young wife had bolder thoughts than this;
She would not lose that promised farewell kiss;
And so she nursed her little babe to rest,
Fixed him securely in his cradle nest,
Caught the young horse, in pastures roaming free,
Now antic with his new found liberty;
Bridled and saddled him with ready hand,
And made him subject to her swift command;
Fastened the house, and mounting on his back,
With her choice bundle took the well-known track;
Sped o'er the hills along the rocky way,
And reached the place where the encampment lay.
It was the rosy, verdant month of June,
A hot and sultry summer afternoon;
Brief was the parting—priceless though but brief,
And the full heart had found a sweet relief.
As she turned homeward to her lonely nest,
A thunder cloud was rising in the west;
Its distant mutterings sounded in her ear,
Quickened her speed and chilled her soul with fear.
Not half her journey had as yet been done,
When the dark clouds shut off the cheerful sun,
And bursting bolts amid the tempest played,
Till horse and rider were like afraid.
Next came the driving wind and drenching rain,
And the fierce tempest swept o'er hill and plain.
But never yet a thunder gust so wild
To keep an anxious mother from her child;
She only saw that lonely cradle bed,
And through the storm with quicker pace she sped,

Till at her gate she dropped the slackened rein,
Took a quick peep through the small window-pane,
And all was right. There still and snug and warm,
Untroubled by the tumult of the storm,
Her babe was sleeping, and her soul at rest;
The winds might howl along the troubled west,
But light would rise and better days impart;
And she had felt the beatings of that heart,
Bound to her own in love's most sacred tie,
And she would wait till those sad years went by.
This is one record from that ancient past,
With no dark clouds nor shadows overcast.
The years moved on—the tempests moved away,
And brought again the brighter better day.
That stout young farmer and his prudent wife
Lived through long years of their laborious life;
That sleeping babe was but the first-born child
Of a long line, this mother's care beguiled.

  And now unto the Lord our God,
   All might and power belong;
  His was the everlasting strength,
   That made our fathers strong;
  As on an eagle's mighty wings,
   Through storms and toils untold,
  He lifted them and carried them,
   Through all those days of old.

  And as the rolling years shall pass,
   And new born ages rise,
  As other generations look
   Upon these hills and skies;

Let them behold Thy glory, Lord,
And follow Thy commands,
So shall the land we love, become
The wonder of all lands.

CHURCH OF OLD WINDSOR, CONN.

March 30th, 1630—1880.

Roll back the curtains of the years, and let our eyes behold
The distant times, the ancient ways, the sturdy men of old;
Across the stormy deep they came, the forest wilds they trod,
To find a home for liberty, a temple for their God.

They rested by the rocky shore, till shone the western star,
To point them to a fertile vale, a peaceful home afar;
They struggled through the pathless woods, till full before their sight,
Spread the fair valley, broad and green, bathed in its vernal light.

They saw the river flowing by, fed from its ancient rills,
Bearing its wealth of waters down from the far northern hills;
In silence and in solitude for ages it had flowed,
To make these lowlands beautiful, most meet for man's abode.

And now they heard the voice of God, as Israel heard
    of old,
Saying: Be strong and fear ye not, let all your hearts
    be bold,
This swelling Jordan ye shall pass beneath my guiding
    hand,
And here your weary feet shall rest, within this goodly
    land.

The Lord thy God He giveth thee this land of brooks
    and rills,
Of fountains and of depths that spring from valleys
    and from hills;
A land of barley and of wheat, of corn and wine and oil,
In plenty shalt thou eat thy bread, upon this fruitful
    soil.

When thou hast eaten and art full, then shalt thou bow
    the knee,
And bless the Lord for this good land He giveth unto
    thee:
Let not thy heart be lifted up in boastful pride to say,
Mine own right hand hath gotten me the wealth I share
    to-day.

Thou shalt remember all the way the Lord thy God
    hath led,
To point thy pathway through the sea, through deserts
    wild and dread;
If thou forsake the Lord thy God, His favor He will
    hide,
And thou, like nations gone before, shalt perish in thy
    pride.

What brought these way-worn wanderers, these weary
    households here,
So far from home and kindred ties and all they held
    most dear?
What nerved their hearts to cross the sea and tread
    this forest path,
To brave the hungry beasts of prey,—the savage in his
    wrath?

A tyrant king had risen up to rule with iron rod;
A haughty priest had strode between their consciences
    and God:
To haughty priest or tyrant king, they would not bend
    the knee;
Come exile, chains or prison walls, their souls should
    still be free!

Such was the cup of bitterness our fathers had to drink,
Such was the penal doom prepared for men who dared
    to think;
So was the good seed sifted out by God's mysterious
    hand,
To plant this empire of the west, this joy of many a land.

And now behold these exiles here, John Warham and
    his flock,
Made up of good old English names, and good old
    English stock;
They come with hearts that trust in God, and hands
    made strong for toil,
To build their rude and humble homes and break the
    waiting soil.

They clustered on this rising ground, where now their
    ashes rest,
They saw the valley's outmost bounds, the blue hills
    east and west;
The little river at their feet in quiet murmured by.
And the great river, broad and deep, lay full before their
    eye.

The dusky children of the woods were glancing to and
    fro,
With faces like the mystic sphinx, whose meaning none
    might know;
They thronged about these river lands, they wandered
    by the streams,
The rambled through the forest paths and dreamed their
    forest dreams.

They sowed these broad and fertile fields with arrow-
    heads and spears,
A harvest for the farmer-boys to crop in after years;
The plough-share still shall turn them up, while cen-
    turies roll apace,
Or sifting winds, on sandy knolls, make bare their
    hiding-place.

And not their arrow-heads alone, their ancient names
    are found,
Still clinging to the modern soil in all the region round;
Podunk and old Poquonnoc, Scantic and Scitico
Recall to us that dusky race that vanished long ago.

But who shall paint those earliest years and bring their dark to light,—
The heavy burdens of the day, the watches of the night?
Those nights when mothers dared not close their weary eyes to rest,
But clasped their babes with every noise more closely to their breast.

The first foundations were not laid when war's wild notes were heard,
And dire alarm and tragic fear through every household stirred,
And well the stoutest heart might quail, the boldest hold their breath,
A bloody challenge had been given,—its issue, life or death.

But soon the black cloud rolled away, the bright sun shone again,
When crowned with victory homeward came John Mason and his men.
That bloody Pequot race was gone, had perished past recall;
The infant towns kept jubilee, in gladness o'er its fall.

Their Indian neighbors too were glad, and danced with forest mirth,
For now their hateful cruel foe was blotted from the earth:
The good news run along the shore to Plymouth and the Bay,
And all New England joined to keep a glad Thanksgiving Day.

In modern "piping times of peace" around their genial
    fires,
Their puny sons may criticize and harshly judge their
    sires,
But that wild tribe had sowed the wind along its bloody
    path,
And now had reaped the whirlwind in all its direful
    wrath.

The years passed on. The little one became a thousand
    strong,
The small one stretched its growing length, the river
    sides along,
The gloomy shadows disappeared before the woodman's
    blows,
The wilderness began to bloom and blossom as the rose.

They sowed and reaped, they bought and sold, they
    wedded and were wed,
The gray-haired fathers passed away, and children rose
    instead;
The catechism taught them all about The Moral Plan,
And every little child could tell the chiefest end of man.

Their tools were rough, their gains were small, but still
    with courage stout,
They taxed themselves in every war to help old Eng-
    land out:
They fought the Indians and the French on many a
    stubborn field,
They fought the Saybrook Platform too, and made the
    clergy yield.

And when Sir Andros came in state, to take their
    charter back,
The lights went out, the charter too, and none could tell
    its track;
When Andros left for Boston town, defeated in his
    plan,
'Tis safe to say he rode away a madder, wiser man.

They fired the Primer at him too—they taught the boys
    to say
Those rhymes about the *Royal Oak* in quite another
    way.
His *Royal Majesty* was dropt, and by a rendering free,
The Charter Oak it was that saved the *People's Liberty.*

Then came the news that James had gone—last of those
    Stuart Kings;
The joyful tale flew o'er the land, as on an eagle's
    wings;
The modest charter ventured out from its dark hiding-
    place,
And for a hundred years shed down its mild benignant
    grace.

Beneath its just and peaceful sway the people dwelt
    secure;
Their Governors were righteous men, their magistrates
    were pure:
They did not look across the sea to wait the royal nod—
They chose for office whom they would, their chartered
    rights were broad.

And so the strange thing came to pass, in seventeen
    seventy-five,*
That Brother Jonathan was found head of the patriot
    hive;
In all the thirteen colonies, no Governor but he
Was ranged upon the people's side, a friend of liberty.

The women of the olden times were busy as the men,
For home-made clothes and household cares were all in
    order then;
The maidens spun the fleecy wool, the mothers spun the
    flax,
What time the men folks were abroad and busy with
    the axe.

The big wheel and the little wheel kept up their buzzing
    sound,
Till all the yearly stock was spun, and all the yarn was
    wound,
And then the pounding loom began, beneath each rustic
    roof,
With flying shuttle to and fro, to join the warp and
    woof.

---

* At the breaking out of the Revolutionary War, in 1775, Jonathan Trumbull, of Lebanon, was Colonial Governor of Connecticut, having been in office since 1769, and continuing till 1783. By the Charter of Connecticut, obtained by the younger John Winthrop in 1662 from Charles II., England held no veto on the action of the people in their choice of Governor. In the other Colonies generally the Governors were of foreign appointment, and, of course, were with the King. But Gov. Trumbull was with the people; and Washington, when in doubt, used, it is said, to remark, "We must see what Brother Jonathan will say." Hence the term "Brother Jonathan."

And many a Windsor lad at Yale, some Ellsworth,
    Rockwell, Stiles,
A Wolcott or an Edwards boy, begirt with ladies' smiles,
Has mounted up to speak his piece upon Commencement
    Day,
Proud in his brand-new suit of clothes, made in this
    simple way.

The ruddy maidens of those years, had they been bought
    and sold,
If judged by any modern rate, were worth their weight
    in gold;
No foreign Bridgets can be hired to do as much as
    they,
Who did it all for kindred love and in a filial way.

What though their hands were hard with toil, with
    household work and care,
No worthier damsels could be found man's destinies to
    share;
For they could fill whatever place unto their lot might
    fall,
And give to life a dignity in cottage or in hall.

Great was the old Town-meeting day, and high was the
    debate,
Touching the questions which arose of Town, or
    Church, or State;
To build a bridge or meeting-house, the voters were
    the same,
Only the latter clause came in under the Parish name.

And great was old Election Day, and great was 'lection cake,
No nourishment for growing boys a prouder seat could take.
Greatest of all, Thanksgiving day; that glad day of the [year,
When roaring fires and chicken-pie filled every house with cheer.

What bard shall sing, in fitting strains, the olden district school?
The benches small and benches big,—the master's wooden rule?
The meaning glances round the room, which passed and made no noise,
The nascent loves that grew and died among the girls and boys:

The spelling-school on winter nights,—the clatter and the din
Which raged before the hour had come for spelling to begin:
The hard words flying to and fro to knock the dunces [down,
The bright-eyed girl or bright-eyed boy that waited for the crown:

The plain old-fashioned meeting-house, with square and pen-like pews:
Where winter cold was kept condensed, all prime for Sunday use:
The tything-man that sat in state on some high gallery perch,
Who rattled round and made more noise than all the boys in church:

The minister who stood aloft in pulpit quaint and tall,
Above his head a sounding-board, which seemed about
    to fall:
The chorister, who gave the pitch and led the waiting
    choir,
Beating the time with outspread arms to lend the need-
    ful fire:

The singing-school to teach the youth the mysteries of
    song,
When young men saw the maidens home and made the
    journey long:
The sleigh-ride on a moonlight night, the passage out
    and back,
When jingling bells on frosty air gave note to clear the
    track.

But time would fail us to pursue this airy, trifling strain,
And so, in parting, let us take our sober song again:
For though life everywhere puts on its playful, sunny
    side,
In earnest thoughts and earnest deeds our fathers lived
    and died.

Let us upraise that olden song,—the ancient psalm once
    more,
Which first our fathers sang when they had reached
    New England's shore;
Let us with voice and heart unite before our fathers'
    God,
That He would give us strength to tread the ways the
    fathers trod,

Thou, Lord, hast been our dwelling-place ere mountain
    tops were reared.
Before the rolling earth was shaped, or ancient hills
    appeared;
Through countless generations past Thy goings were
    abroad,
From everlasting is Thy name,—the ever-living God.

Thou turnest man again to dust, frail child of earth and
    clay,
While in Thy sight a thousand years are counted but a
    day;
To Thee the ages come and go, in never-ending flight,
As yesterday when it is past, or as a watch by night.

Our days are three-score years and ten, or, if Thou givest
    strength,
So that they reach to four-score years, how weary is
    their length!
For heavy burdens clog their path, and sorrows cloud
    their way,
And soon, how soon, the day is done, we haste and fly
    away!

So teach us, Lord, to count our days, daily to grow more
    wise,
And let Thy glorious work appear before our children's
    eyes;
The beauty of the Lord our God, upon us may it rest,
That all the labor of our hands may be confirmed and
    blest.

ABSALOM.

The smooth-faced demagogue—behold he waits,
    Watching, with restless eye, the busy throngs
Press in and outward, at the city gates,
    To catch the men who have some fancied wrongs;
With knowing wink, he beckons them aside,
    And hears, with pitying look, their tales of grief,
Asks for their homes and children—feeds their pride,
    And hopes devoutly they may find relief.

"David, my father, now is growing old,
    And things are out of joint beneath his reign;
Taxes are high—there's too much liquor sold,
    On every side I hear the folks complain:
I have no taste for scenes of public strife,
    But still, if people want me for their king,
I *could* forego the charms of private life
    And to the office some small talent bring.

"Not for myself do I desire the place,
    'Tis for the people only I would serve;
To work reforms amid such dire disgrace
    Requires, I know, considerable nerve;
David has bad advisers in his court,—
    There's Nathan, Joab, Zadok and the rest,
Who use their offices for gain and sport,—
    I would break up this old and filthy nest.

"Not for myself should I approach the throne;
   I feel" (he drops a tear) "for all your woes."
(He hides his face, and tries to hide a groan,
   While his breast heaves with sympathetic throes)
So after months of this mock sympathy,
   The wily leader hies him to his den,
Rings out old Israel's ancient battle-cry,
   And round him flock all discontented men.

From hills and vales these men of fancied wrong
   Come trooping in, in many a straggling band,
And day by day the host is waxing strong,
   While storm and revolution fill the land:
Spirits of evil fly upon the air,
   The aged monarch trembles on his throne,
The timid wring their hands in mute despair,
   And the new upstart calls the hour his own.

But soon march forth King David's men of war
   With their bold captain firmly at their head,
And with one stroke—one sharp, quick battle-jar—
   This wild revolt within the realm is dead;
The cunning leader, forced in haste to flee,
   In riding by an oak, too near the limb,
His nice, long hair gets tangled in the tree,
   And this same Joab does the job for him.

HOW I FIRST WENT DOWN TO YALE.

Listen, my comrades, while I tell
    The old and time-worn tale,
What, in the years long gone, befell,
    When I first went down to Yale;
When things went on, about as well,
    On quite a different scale.

'Twas in the month of August,
    A hot and sultry day,
I set out with my minister,
    All in his "one hoss shay,"
And o'er the hills and plains we took
    Our solitary way.

We left a good old country town,
    With pastures large and green,
Where meadows wet, and uplands dry,
    Diversified the scene,
And where the old farm-houses
    In comely rows were seen.

South by south-west we took our course,
    And held our steady way,
To reach that fair and sunny plain
    Whereon New Haven lay,
With her two mountains standing guard,
    To keep all foes away.

ENTERING YALE.

At twelve, as we could plainly tell
    By sound of country clocks,
We made a halt to eat our lunch,
    Among the shady rocks,
And gave our horse a peck of oats
    We carried in the box.

And when the sun, all burning red,
    Was sinking in the west,
And our tired beast, that certainly
    Had done his "level best,"
Began to hint, by many signs,
    That he desired to rest;

We came upon that ridge of land
    Which overlooks the Bay,
And on my eager vision burst
    Ten thousand stacks of hay;
A sight more new and wonderful
    Than any seen that day.

But when we reached New Haven town,
    And saw its wondrous green,
And when those time-worn college halls
    Just westerly were seen,
The thoughts I had within my breast
    Were mighty thoughts, I ween.

The place was full of life and stir,
    The streets were glad and gay,
Young men and maidens walked abroad,
    Clad in their best array,
And every thing was ripening
    For an old Commencement Day.

And when the hazy moon-beams fell
　　Through the still evening air,
'Twas like a dream of ancient rest,
　　Far off from sin and care;
The world was clothed in beauty,
　　Like Eden, bright and fair.

O days of youth! when fancy wakes,
　　And clothes the earth in light,
When all the future stands arrayed
　　In colors warm and bright,
Would that the world could look once more
　　Just as it looked that night!

In the calm gathering twilight,
　　That evening, might be seen
A youngster, walking forth alone,
　　With reverential mien,
Though others might describe him
　　As "a wearing of the green."

Along the front of college yard,
　　With thoughtful step and slow,
In the soft silvery moonlight
　　He wandered to and fro,
Until a chap came gliding up
　　He did not chance to know.

"I take you for a Freshman, Sir!
　　If I may judge by sight,
And I have a curiosity
　　To know if all is right.
Pray tell, with what Society
　　You purpose to unite?

"If to the Brothers you incline,
　　Or harbor such a thought,
I tell you, Sir, upon my word,
　　That you had better not:
They've got an awful debt to pay,
　　For those nice things they bought.

"The only safe Society
　　Is Old Linonia;
She is older than the Brothers,
　　Yes Sir! by many a day,
And she's got a splendid brand-new desk,　.
　　And not a cent to pay.

"Just mark the College Faculty,
　　All of its chiefest men,
Those who can think the deepest,
　　And those who use the pen:
They joined with Old Linonia,
　　And would do the same again."

I thanked the young man kindly,
　　For all the light he shed,
I knew all this was true before,.
　　Yes, every word he said;
That very day, my minister
　　Had lodg'd this in my head.

Scarce had this fellow vanished
　　Across the college green,
When up there came another chap
　　Of more ferocious mien;
Some saucy Sophs were just behind
　　To see, what might be seen.

"About this Bully question, Sir!
    On which side do you vote?
Is your opinion all made up,
    Or are you still afloat?
Just make a statement, if you please,
    And let me make a note.

"Are you aware that Bullyism
    Came down from ages hoary?
That by it Yale is what she is,
    With all her ancient glory?
Go ask the College Faculty,
    They'll tell you the same story.

"If you don't vote for Bully,
    I give you warning true,
There are some chaps about here
    To take and put you through.
You'll find Old Yale a hotter place,
    Than Tophet ever knew."

Off through the dreamy moonlight,
    This stormy fellow goes,
While those five Sophs behind him,
    Put their thumbs unto their nose,
And so the interview was brought
    To a successful close.

Once more, my ancient comrades,
    Come, listen unto me,
On one point, I am very sure,
    We all of us agree;
Things now are very different
    From what they used to be.

ENTERING YALE.

For when we entered College,
 We all remember well,
How mightily the Tutors
 Did common men excel;
And how by size and look and walk
 A Senior we could tell.

But now, at Yale you cannot know
 A Senior from a Soph;
You only tell a Tutor,
 By seeing hats go off:
So great the change you feel, at heart,
 Inclined to laugh and scoff.

Yes, Tutors, Seniors, Juniors, Sophs,
 Are all so much the same,
You walk about, in musing mood,
 And inwardly exclaim,
Where are those old distinctions gone?
 And what is College fame?

The age has grown degenerate;
 We never more shall hear
Such grand and lofty orators,
 With voices ringing clear,
As those we heard in College halls,
 Back in our Freshman year.

We may not hope to see again
 Men so august and great,
Men of such manly stature
 And of such high estate,
As were the Seniors when we passed
 In at the College gate.

ANGLO-SAXON WHITTLING SONG.

"Your Yankee is always to be found with a jack knife, and when he has nothing else to do, is eternally whittling."—*Growling old Traveller.*

In the olden time of England, the days of Norman pride,
The mail-clad chieftain buckled on his good sword at his side,
And mounted on his trusty steed, from land to land he strayed,
And ever as he wandered on, he whittled with his blade.
  O those foolish days of whittling!

He was out in search of monsters—of giants grim and tall,
He was hunting up the griffins—the dragons great and small,
He broke in through the oak doors of many a castle gate,
And what he whittled when within, 'tis needless to relate.
  O those foolish days of whittling!

But when the pomp of feudal pride like a dream had passed away,
And every where the knightly steel was rusting to decay,

The common-people drew their blades in quite another cause,
And in the place of giants grim, they whittled up the laws.
  O those stern old days of whittling!

They whittled down the royal throne with all its ancient might,
And many a tough old cavalier was whittled out of sight;
They whittled off the king's head, and set it on the wall,
They whittled out a commonwealth, but it could not last at all.
  O those fiery days of whittling!

There came across the stormy deep, a stern and iron band,
A solemn look on every face—their hatchets in their hand,
They whittled down the forest oak, the chestnut and the pine,
And planted in the wilderness the rose-tree and the vine.
  O those fearful days of whittling!

They made themselves a clearing, and housed their little freight,
Then put their Sunday coats on, and whittled out a state,
They cut it round so perfectly, they whittled it so "true,"
That it still stands in beauty for all the world to view.
  O those grand old days of whittling!

When England sent her hirelings, with cannon, gun and
    blade,
To break and batter down the State, which these good
    men had made,
The people seized for weapons whatever came to hand,
And whittled these intruders back and drove them
    from the land.
        O the heroic days of whittling!

In men of Saxon blood it stays—this love of whittling
    —still,
And something must be whittled, to pacify the will.
When the old wars were over, and peace came back
    again,
They took to whittling mountains, and filling vale and
    glen.
        O those peaceful days of whittling!

They whittled out the railroad path, thro' hill and rock
    and sand,
And sent their snorting engines in thunder through the
    land;
Sails whitened all the harbors, the mountain valleys
    stirred,
And the hum and roar of labor through all the land was
    heard.
        O those busy days of whittling!

But there long had dwelt among us a gaunt and hideous
    Wrong,
Set round with ancient guarantees, with legal ramparts
    strong;

With look and tone defiant, it feared not God or man,
But snatched on every side for power to work its wick-
    ed plan,—
        All ripe and dry for whittling!

Of old this Wrong was humble, asking with pious cry,
This only, to be left alone, in its own time to die;
But fed by this first yielding, bolder and bolder grown,
Shameless before the nations now, it reared its bloody
        throne;
        The time draws nigh for whittling!

"Pride goes before destruction," the wise man said of
    old,
"Whom the gods seek to ruin they first make mad,"
    and bold;
In the frenzy of its madness, this Wrong forgot its place,
Came out with noise of gongs to fright our Yankee
        whittling race.
        God gave this chance for whittling!

And now my trusty Saxons, who came from near and
    far,
Remember who your fathers were, and set your teeth
    for war;
"Sword of the Lord and Gideon," be still your battle-
    cry,
And strike as Samson struck of old, smite Slavery hip
    and thigh;
        Now is your time for whittling!

And when the land shall rest again from all this noise
   and strife,
And Peace her olive-branch shall wave o'er this broad
   realm of life,
Fair as the sun, our nation before the world shall stand,
Freedom on all her banners, freedom throughout the
   land.
      O these grand rewards of whittling!

GOLDEN WEDDINGS.

I.

1820—1870.

We gather on this festive night,
  And send our memories back,
To bring again the vanished years
  Along life's misty track;
To call to mind the by-gone days—
  "Those good old times"—you know,
When all was grand, and pure and true,
  Just fifty years ago.

We gather in this happy home,
  This dear parental nest;
Which, through the sunshine and the storm,
  Our Father's love has blest:

We count the sorrows and the joys
  In life's unceasing flow,
    Back to the hour this home began,
  Just fifty years ago.

The men and women of that age
  Were hearty, strong and bold;
They went to meeting,—stayed all day,—
  Through sternest winter cold:
They sat and rapped their aching feet,
  To make the warm blood flow;
They blew their frozen finger-ends,
  Just fifty years ago.

One of the questions of that time,
  O'er which debate waxed hot,
Was that great question, fresh and new,
  To have a stove or not;
" Our fathers used no stoves in church,
  Then why should we do so"?
That was the way they looked at things
  Just fifty years ago.

Our *fathers* used no stoves in church,
  But still our *mothers* did;
Those little square tin boxes,
  In which the fire was hid:
To keep the maids and matrons warm,
  These stoves passed to and fro,
While tougher men and boys went cold,
  Just fifty years ago.

Then, at the church, the preacher stood,
   Perched high against the wall,
With the huge sounding-board above,
   Which seemed about to fall:
With overcoat and mittens on,
   To keep him in a glow,
He whiled away the wintry hour,
   Just fifty years ago.

And when he took his walks abroad,
   Men paused as he went by,
To pay a graceful courtesy,
   And look with reverent eye;
And school-boys, as they saw him come,
   Arranged themselves in row,
And made him their profoundest bow,
   Just fifty years ago.

Those square, high-backed, old-fashioned pews,
   With open work about,   [heads,
Through which small boys could push their
   But could not pull them out:
We shall not see the like again,
   Wherever we may go;
They're lost and gone—those queer old pews
   Of fifty years ago.

To keep awake, in summer time,
   We helped the feeble will,
By eating generous quantities
   Of fennel and of dill:

Or to the woods, in pious crowds,
    We used at noon to go,
And pick the fresh young wintergreen,
    Just fifty years ago.

Up stairs, on one side, sat the girls,
    On one side sat the boys,
They sometimes caught each other's eyes,
    But did not make a noise;
They were afraid they might wake up
    The old folks, down below;
That was the way boys looked at things
    Just fifty years ago.

If there are any modern boys,
    Who happen here to-night,
To hear about those good old times
    When all the boys did right;
As soon as they have heard the tale,
    I want them all to go,
And imitate those noble boys
    Of fifty years ago.

* * * * * *

Enough, enough, those good old times
    Deserve a tenderer strain,
For then, as now, earth's purest joys
    Were mixed with keenest pain;
And youthful eyes, that then shone bright,
    With radiant hope aglow,
In all their light, were quenched in death,
    Back, fifty years ago.

How many, on the right and left,
  Have dropt their heavy load,
And vanished from our mortal sight,
  Along life's weary road!
We are but strangers on the earth,
  And pilgrims here below,
We journey, as our fathers did,
  Just fifty years ago.

For all God's care and kindness, shown
  To this long-wedded pair,
We here record our gratitude,
  In humble praise and prayer;
In all the years of life, we walk
  In ways we do not know,—
So is it now, and so it was
  In the long years ago.

This world is not our resting-place;
  We tarry but a day;
The fair and shining shores, we seek,
  Though near, seem far away;
The crowding generations come,
  And generations go,
And life and death are mingled still,
  As fifty years ago.

GOLDEN WEDDINGS.

II.

1824—1874.

Let gladsome songs go up to-night,
   And household altars burn,
For round us falls a golden light,
   And festal days return:
     No day is like that olden day,
       That shines on us from far,
     When hope was rising o'er our way,
       Like some bright morning star.

As we look back through joy and pain,
   Along the misty years,
Our pleasant memories rise again,
   And trouble disappears:
     No day is like that olden day,
       When life was fresh and strong,
     And hearts sang out their happy lay,
       As birds their morning song.

And what has earth more sweet and fair,
   Or more like heaven above,
Than those pure pleasures which we share,
   In ways of household love?
     No day is like that olden day,
       When love first shed its light,
     And spread around our earthly way
       Its colors warm and bright.

The children's hearts are here to-night,
  And children's children sing,
They make this service their delight,
  And grateful offerings bring:
    No day is like that olden day,
      When sheltered in the nest,
    Our mother sang her cradle lay,
      And hushed our griefs to rest.

We look along the lengthened years,
  Along the pathway trod,
In all the journey there appears
  The guiding hand of God:
    No day is like that olden day,
      When bending low in prayer,
    Amid the perils of the way,
      We sought a Father's care.

III.

1825—1875.

It was when the birds were singing,
  And the woods with music ringing,
    When bedecked with summer glory,
      Fields and meadows lay in bloom;
When the sun had just completed
That round course which God has meted,
    And stood poised in tropic splendor
      Scattering all the northern gloom:

Then a young man and a maiden,
With life's hopes and promise laden,
   Full of dreams and gentle visions
     Such as only youth can know;
Stood before the bridal altar,
And with lips that did not falter,
   Took the vows of God upon them,
     Hand in hand, through life to go.

Thus their mutual love they plighted,
And, to-day, with hands united,
   Children's children gathering round them,
     Here before their God they stand;
From that goal, whence thus they started,
Fifty winters have departed,
   And the pilgrimage draws nearer,
     Nearer to the border land.

Day by day, their God has led them,
Day by day, has clothed and fed them,
   Kept them in the storm and tempest,
     Through the dangers of the way;
Now their hearts, though tinged with sadness,
Lift on high their songs of gladness,
   That kind heaven to them has granted
     To behold this joyous day.

O how sweet these memories olden!
When the future bright and golden
   Beckoned as with outstretched finger,
     Bid us haste to taste its joy;

When the pulse of youth was bounding,
And our hearts with joy resounding,
　Nature played and danced before us,
　　And our life knew no alloy.

Now though many a hope be blasted,
Many a dream which we forecasted;
　Though the way has oft been weary,
　　And the burdens hard to bear:
Out of pain and toil and sorrow,
God doth make this bright to-morrow,
　And we would not change the journey
　　Which we make beneath His care.

Life is richer, broader, deeper,
To the sad and patient weeper,
　Than to him who knows no sorrow,
　　Walking ever in the light:
As, when storms are disappearing,
And the clouds are lifting, clearing,
　Sunset comes with fuller glory,
　　As the day descends to night.

Simple is that olden story,
Of the years now pale and hoary,
　When the church, the farm, the school-house,
　　Made the round of country life;
When amid these northern mountains,
By these cool clear hillside fountains,
　Lonely households lived and labored,
　　Far from noise and city strife.

* * * * * * * *

Say ye not that life is barren;
Sweeter than the rose of Sharon
  Are the memories that cluster
    Round a life in honor spent;
Bright with an immortal beauty
Is a long life, linked to duty,
  Ever toiling and aspiring,
    In a patient sweet content.

With sincerest salutations,
With our heart-felt gratulations,
  We would bring our gifts and honors,
    At this happy festive hour;
Glad that we have been invited,
Thus to crown these heads united,
  And for their remaining journey
    Crave God's kind protecting care.

IV.

1832—1882.

Since the glad marriage bell rang out its sound,
  With merry notes to cheer the festive crowd,
How many gliding months have seen their round,
  Through changing scenes of sunshine and of cloud!

O long-gone day of early love and light,
  When fancy shed her soft romantic gleams,
When with strong step we climbed the mountain height,
  And nought could break our sweet and golden dreams.

Now once again, in sober ripened years,
  The happy pair stand here before their God,
Their eyes suffused with warm and grateful tears,
  As they look back along the pathway trod.

And now, O Father! give their pilgrim feet,
  Firmness and strength for the remaining way,
Guide them through wintry storms and summer heat,
  Till they shall reach the glad eternal day!

SILVER WEDDING.

1845—1870.

They say that once in seven years,
  Be the time less or greater,
For systems have their laws of change,
  Some earlier and some later;
Once in seven years then, as a rule,
  The art called vaccination
Requires to be done over,
  For its own preservation.

It happens in this round of years,
  The power gets so abated,
The only safe way is to go
  And be re-vaccinated;

SILVER WEDDING.

Thus the old virtue is restored,
    The former force imparted;
And the same influence lives again,
    As fresh as when it started.

It has been found in modern days
    The same law holds in marriage,
And this we state, with no intent
    To slander or disparage:
But in this world of wear and tear,
    Where all is fading, dying,
The nuptial knot, from time to time,
    Itself requires re-tying.

So there are many wedding days,
    Besides that ancient first one,—
In fact, upon a full survey,
    That may be called the worst one;
The system takes its start from that,
    And with an upward taper,
It reaches next the wedding day
    Known in the books as paper.

Then comes, with some small lapse of years,
    That wooden institution,
Which brings the pails and washtubs in,
    In rich and large profusion;
Yea more, as Tennyson has sung
    In his enchanting number,
It sometimes fiddles in the trees
    For firewood and for lumber.

SILVER WEDDING.

Of all the weddings I have seen,
    Commend me to a tin one;
It sets the shining things about,
    All in a way to win one;
There is no earthly day so bright,
    At least so far as I know,
Except those days which bring the *tin*,
    Known at the banks as *rhino*.

Then follows on, in order due,
    Our silver wedding season,
Which comes in what Tom Paine, perhaps,
    Might call "The Age of Reason;"
And when long years have passed away,
    And life grows gray and olden,
Then comes the solemn marriage day,
    The wedding day called GOLDEN.

Those are the days when married pairs,
    Once more rejuvenated,
Go on their way again, in strength
    Confirmed and reinstated;
They catch again the radiant gleam
    Of all that far-off glory,—
They hear again, in tender tones,
    The old bewitching story.

* * * * * * *

And now to all unmarried men,
    Of every class and station,
I wish to speak one earnest word,
    By way of application:

If you expect, in course of years,
  To reach a silver wedding,
You must regard first principles,
  The tables, chairs and bedding.

"Order is heaven's first law"—so sang
  A famous olden poet;
And all we learn of human life
  Helps to confirm and show it.
These pleasant after-wedding days,
  A wooden or a tin one,
How can you ever hope to see,
  Unless you dare begin one?

JACKSON FALLS, N. H.—AND OLD DOG SPRING.

1866.

Don't let me forget to make mention
  Of Old Spring, that lives near the Falls,
And gives his politest attention
  To wait on the stranger who calls.

As the men are all busy with haying,
  And the women are cooking the trout,
Old Spring cocks his eye to you, saying,
  You see there is some one about.

OLD DOG SPRING.

I am ready to wait on you now, Sir,
   I will show you the Falls, if you please,
I will give you my choicest bow-wow, Sir,
   While you stroll about at your ease.

Old Spring, how he waits on the stranger!
   Now he chit-chats along by his side,
Now he barks, to scare away danger,
   Or runs on before as a guide.

Yes, Spring is a funny old fellow,
   Not half of his wit can be told;
He can out-rival old Punchinello,
   He has rare tricks yet to unfold.

He goes to attack a small stone, Sir,
   That lies half way up in the glen;
Goes boldly—he goes all alone, Sir,
   This wonder of dogs and of men.

From the bed where it snugly reposes,
   He has dragged his old enemy out;
And now in fierce conflict he closes,
   And makes the hills ring with his shout.

And now he comes back for your greeting,
   With victory gained at the last,
O the wonder and joy of that meeting!
   These dangers successfully passed.

You must treat him with consideration;
   You must quiet his quick-beating heart;
You must lend him your high approbation,
   So well has he acted his part.

So let all our enemies perish!
　　As that stone went down to the deep;
But such valor we ever will cherish,
　　And the record we ever shall keep.

Then sing we the fame and the glory
　　Of Old Spring, that lives near the Falls,
And tell to our children the story,
　　How he waits on the stranger that calls.

A CHANGE OF THE MOON.

A PLAIN, clever man is my neighbor Gray,
　　And we often take counsel together;
He lives in a farm-house over the way,
　　And is wise in respect to the weather;
He watches all signs, night, morning, and noon,
But pins his great faith on a change of the moon.

In the dull, drizzly May, when the signs were all bad,
　　And, day after day, it kept raining,
When the farmers were sad, and the women were mad,
　　And all the wide world was complaining;
Farmer Gray went on piping the very same tune,
"It will never clear off till a change of the moon."

I admired his great faith, for the east wind blew strong,
　　From icebergs and isles of the ocean,
The moon had changed thrice, while the storm kept along,

A CHANGE OF THE MOON.

But my neighbor still stuck to his notion;
At length it cleared up, near the coming of June,
Two days and a half from a change of the moon!

In the long summer drought, when the springs had run
    Not a sign of a rain-cloud appearing,   [dry,
Neighbor Gray, who knew the wherefore and why,
    Spake out, and his accents were cheering:
"We are bound to have different weather soon,
For to-morrow, you know, there's a change of the moon."

I sit by his fire, on a sharp winter night,
    When the glass below zero is ranging;
My neighbor instructs me with honest delight
    (For his faith in the moon is unchanging),
That a thaw will set in by Saturday noon,
For just at that time comes a change of the moon.

Heat and cold, wet and dry, or whatever the grief
    Under which our poor earth may be lying,
Neighbor Gray knows the source whence must come our
    No use of this groaning and sighing;   [relief;
He tells all he meets that a change will come soon,
"We must wait, my dear friends, till a change of the moon."

He cares not a jot for the college or school,
    And passes their doings unheeded,
Still he holds by the old philosophical rule,
    To name no more causes than needed;
And as one is enough, the rest let us prune,
And make all things proceed from a change of the moon.

REVOLUTIONARY TEA.

Dec. 18, 1773—1873.

A song to-night, and a legend,
  A story often told,
Of the brave New England fathers,
  In the stormy days of old;
A tale of the things that happened
  In seventeen seventy-three.
They chose that year so it might rhyme
  With tea, and sea, and free,
  With jollity and glee,
And with that large and glorious word,
  A nation's liberty.

Those men were wise and thoughtful,
  They saw a coming day,
A grand good time for speech and rhyme
  A century away;
And they knew that all the poets
  Must make their wordy rounds,
And fill their lines out merrily,
  With harmony of sounds.
  They saw that this would be
  In eighteen seventy-three,
And so they had compassion
  On working-men like me.

REVOLUTIONARY TEA.

Yes, those were thoughtful Mohawks,
    For they took a hearty lunch,
And fortified the carnal man
    With good old whiskey punch;
And thoughtfully they started out,
    And took the nearest way,
By street and block, to Griffin's dock,
    Where the good ship Dartmouth lay,
    In the quiet Boston Bay,
And then with speed they did the deed
    We celebrate to-day.

The business which they had in hand,
    'Twas needful to despatch it,
And so they had at their command,
    Each one a little hatchet;
They broke the chests in thoughtfully,
    And emptied out the p'ison
And gave the harbor such a dose
    Of Souchong and of Hyson,
That when that tea had time to steep,
Our matters could not go to sleep,
In fact that dose woke up the deep,
    And stirred the far horizon.

Yes, those were thoughtful Mohawks;
    When their evening's work was done
They hied them to their forests,
    Toward the setting sun;
And when the morrow morning dawned,
    In all the city 'round
The search was vain, in street or lane

Not a man of them was found;
For they were not around,—
To their dark western forests
　They had sped them with a bound.

There is an old tradition,
　Of which we here might speak,
How a faint farewell trace was left
　Upon a lady's cheek:
One of those thoughtful Mohawks,
　Ere he was lost to view,
Returned to give a parting kiss
　To a lady whom he knew,
　And he left the red man's hue
　Adhering there like glue;
Then to his native forests
　He thoughtfully withdrew.

Meanwhile the Old South Meeting-House
　Was calling in the people,
The country folks had heard the news,
　Rung from the ancient steeple;
And through the streets and up the aisles
　The surging crowds were swaying,
To find the patriot orators,
　And hear what they were saying,
　And how nicely they were playing,
The harp of thousand strings, the while,
　Their every touch obeying.

But why is all this noise and shout,
　This uproar and confusion?
Are these wild people led about,

Under some strange delusion?
They will not pay John Bull his tax,
   And go unrepresented;
They will no longer bend their backs,
   If it can be prevented;
They cannot live contented,
To moil and toil like servile hacks
   They never have consented.

"I'll tax their tea," King George says he,
   "Because I know what's human,
And think I ought to understand
   The weaknesses of woman;
She loves so much that precious herb
   She can never let it be,
She won't give up the darling drink
   Which I send across the sea;
So we'll lay the tax on tea,
   And lay it rather free;
The woman ever rules the man,
   So trust yourself to me."

The Yankee wives and maids replied,
   "If that be your reliance,
We'll break our tea-pots, every one,
   And bid our king defiance.
We join our brothers in the strife,
   And take the lot that falls;
We are not like those simpering dames,
   That dress your palace walls,
   And tread your courtly halls;
We were not made to come and go,
   Because a tyrant calls.

"This very day, we pack away
  Our nice old china dishes,
And let our choice Young Hyson go
  To feed the hungry fishes;
We join the league, and share the cost,
  Whate'er the future be:
Come weal or woe, come death or life,
  Our souls at least are free,
  And we will not bend the knee,
Your idol for our worship
  We cast it to the sea."

And when the daring deed was done,
  With lightning speed it flew,—
They meant, that day, by "lightning speed,"
  The best a horse could do;
The news, it journeyed north and south,
  It travelled east and west,
It wandered like the wandering Jew
  And found no place of rest,
  But on and on it pressed,
Till it roused the thirteen colonies
  From sea to mountain crest.

So on that day, in Boston bay,
  A stirring deed was done,
Whose fame shall still go sounding on,
  Down to the latest sun;
It was a nation's voice that spoke,
  Across that winter sea,
To tell the tyrant on his throne
  To take back his decree

And let the people be;
And so those sturdy freemen wrought,
That day, for you and me.

THE OLD CHESTNUT TREE.

At the earliest ray of an autumn day,
　In the years of long ago,
In a rocky land where the rough hills stand
　And the noisy rivulets flow;
Willie and Dan, and their wee sister Ann,
　Were out of the snug warm nest,
And off in their glee, to the old chestnut tree,
　That stood on a hill to the west.

Their feet were all bare to the biting air,
　But they counted for little the cost;
And the fields were white in the dawning light,
　With the thick October frost;
They stopt on their way, where the great stones lay,
　With shouting, and frolic, and fun,
For the rocks gave heat to their little red feet,
　From the warmth of yesterday's sun.

The old chestnut tree was a joy to see,
　With its gnarled and rugged form;
It stood in its pride, with its branches thrown wide,
　And had battled with many a storm:

THE OLD CHESTNUT TREE.

Generations of yore had gathered its store,
    In the autumns long gone by,
And the young and brave will sleep in their grave,
    Ere the stout old tree shall die.

With basket and cup, ere the squirrels were up,
    Or the sun had peeped over the hill,
They reached the old tree—and down on the knee
    Were working away with a will:
'Twas a morning of luck, for the sharp frost had struck,
    And opened the fruit to the light;
And at every stir, the nuts from the burr
    Had quietly dropt, through the night.

They forgot their cold feet, and the frosty sleet,
    In the joy of their plentiful store:
For baskets were stuffed, and pockets were puffed,
    And Ann's cup would'nt hold any more;
But Willie and Dan soon hit on a plan,
    And filled their old hats to the full:
It needed some care, for they leaked here and there,
    Where time had eaten the wool.

So they gathered their load, and made for the road,
    Little Ann running hard to keep up;
Her cheek like the rose, when in summer it glows,
    And she carried her own little cup:
But their breakfast was sweet, as they toasted their feet,
    And ate of the doughnuts their fill,
And talked of the luck, which they had for their pluck,
    At the old chestnut tree on the hill.

O give me the joy of the free country boy,
   Who minds not for frost or for snow;
Who climbs the rough hills, and tracks the wild rills,
   And whose blood is kept warm by its flow:
With eyes shining bright, heart cheerful and light,
   He brushes all hardships away,
He is up with the sun, and when labor is done
   He is fresh from his work for his play.

DEDICATION OF A CITY HALL.

To orators, both great and small,
      Of many words, or few,
This ample, well-developed Hall,
From floor to ceiling, wall to wall,
      We dedicate to you.

We seem to hear the high debate,
      Go sounding down the years,
For no American is great,
Who cannot rise and stand and state
      The thing—as it appears.

To whispering lovers, who may come
      Amid this warmth and light,
Because you cannot meet at home,
And find the air too cold to roam
      Upon a winter's night;

We dedicate this Hall to you,
    As rolling years go by,
Your opportunities are few,
Come here and have your interview
    Beneath the public eye.

To active-minded little boys,
    That here their pastime take,
Who, eating peanuts with a noise,
And appetite that never cloys,
    Contrive to keep awake;

The tithing-man is not about,
    He died before your day;
Your brass-tipped shoes are firm and stout,
So clatter in and clatter out,—
    This is your place for play.

To him who wears the creaky boots,
    And comes to lectures late,
Whose taste a front seat only suits,
While speakers stand as still as mutes,
    And for his sitting wait;

To local politicians, too,
    Who love the people well,
Who keep the general good in view,
And tell the voters what to do,
    And how to buy and sell;

Here shape the business of the Ward,
    And help us all you can,

Come gather here with one accord,
For virtue is its own reward,
    And life is but a span.

But while you plan, contrive and fix,
    There's danger on your track,
The gun you carry has its tricks,
When loaded overmuch it kicks,
    And throws its owner back.

To all of these and many more,
    To people great and small,
Here stands for you an open door,
And for your sakes we look before,
    And dedicate this Hall.

BOSTON-OLOGY.

PERHAPS I owe my hearers an apology,
In turning now a moment to theology.

If you would know the wonders of divinity,
You must come down to "Boston and vicinity,"
Where moral systems rise and disappear,
Still fresh and new, a score or two a year,
Launched on the world, all bristling and complete
By what is called "omniscient self-conceit."
One who lives here is privileged to attend
A preachéd gospel, where some Reverend friend,
Still pressing on all mysteries to explore,

Makes some bold push none ever made before;
He goes so fast you sometimes think, indeed,
That he is riding a velocipede.
Come on, then, stranger, go along with me,
Let's to the House of God in company;
With reverence let us heed the Sabbath call,
Which sounds abroad from Horticultural Hall.
This is the land, sir, of the Pilgrim Fathers,
Home of the Chauncys and the Cotton Mathers.
To Horticultural Hall, then, let us go,
Where the fair flowers of sacred rhetoric blow.
Now who stands up the gospel to proclaim,
Should wear, of course, a Reverend to his name;
With this heaven-born appendage, he may teach
Doctrines like those we hear our preacher preach:
" All prayer is folly. Undeveloped souls,
" That linger yet upon the muddy shoals
" Of earthly being, these in prayer may find
" Some feeble comfort, but the higher mind,
" The philosophic man, has no such need,
" Sufficient ever to himself. Indeed
" If he desired to pray, it is not clear
" That there is any one his prayers to hear.
" We dare to ask if that huge personality,
" Which men call God, be shadow or reality."

Now tell me, stranger, ere you take your hat,
Say, did you ever hear the like of that?
Perhaps you don't remember where you be,
For this is Sunday, and the man you see,
Who's been a talking, is the minister;
Nay, spare that doubting look so sharp and sinister,

For aught I know a Doctor of Divinity,
With his old Puritanic consanguinity.
Where, stranger, will you find, go far or near,
Such Christian privilege as we have down here?
Of course you'll come next Sabbath and the next,—
Some will preach with, and some without a text.
To make the whole seem gentle, kind and human,
At times the preaching will be done by woman ;
Firmly by the old Scripture rule we bide,
For Deborah sang and Miriam prophesied :
And when a stricter doctrine we demand,
Some pious layman near will lend a hand.

Next Sabbath comes. Promptly we take our seat,
To lose no crumb of this rich gospel treat.
Another Reverend brother tries to show,
What he from his vocation ought to know:
That the old Christian Faith leads men astray,
That "Free Religion" is the better way.
And if you ask what Free Religion is,
'Tis of a kind, my friend, you cannot miss,
You have it always, whether saint or sinner,
Whether you kill your wife, or eat your dinner;
In fact the mixture can't be spread much thinner.
You look surprised. You don't believe, my friend,
That this man also is a Reverend?
Why certainly he is, 'tis "Sabba-day,"
This is a Christian minister, on pay,
Hired by the people here to preach and pray.

Perchance to try once more, you feel inclined,
And see what farther wonders we can find :

Our preaching here affords a wide variety,
And some uncommon types of modern piety.
We heard one minister and then another,
To-day we have again a Reverend brother:
He rises now—keep still and hear him state
The Christian theme he essays to debate.
"The piety of Pantheism, as displayed
Among the Hindus of the higher grade."

Again the stranger says—you cannot mean
That this is Christian worship where we've been?
Not Christian worship! Pray what is it, then?
Isn't this the Sabbath-day? I ask again;
Isn't that a minister, made such by rule,
A finished product of our neighboring school?
It only proves what I set out to state,
Our Christian privilege down here is great,
We have the gospel in as many dishes
As ought to satisfy a Frenchman's wishes.

If then you have a theologic doubt,
Some knotty point you cannot well make out,
Bring it to Boston, in the winter season,
And get the marvellous light of modern reason
Concentrated on the case. 'Tis certain, very,
The effect will be quite extraordinary.

YALE COLLEGE.

Closing Stanzas of Phi Beta Kappa Poem, at New Haven.
1871.

So leave we now this trifling,
   And touch a soberer strain;
For on these fair and charméd grounds,
   Old thoughts come back again;
The crowding memories gather
   From long departed years,
They touch the heart with tenderness,
   They fill the eyes with tears.

The dead are thronging round us,
   Old comrades true and tried,
With whom in joyous converse
   We climbed the mountain side;
With whom in nights of beauty
   We trod the moonlit shore,
And saw in starry visions
   The years rise up before.

The dead are gathering round us;
   Our teachers, good and wise,
Who opened wisdom's wondrous page
   Before our youthful eyes;

They taught us earthly knowledge,
    Taught us the fear of God,
And kept the two great worlds in view,
    In all the path we trod.

OLD YALE, our dear old mother!
    We love to breathe her name;
We love to tell her noble deeds,
    And sound abroad her fame;
We love her simple story,
    Her modest country ways,
In those old times when she began
    Her progeny to raise.

We trace her early fortunes,
    Her years of sore distress,
While yet the little Commonwealth
    Was a rough wilderness;
While yet the howling savage
    Lurked in his forest den,
And all the towns could not enroll
    Four thousand arméd men.

Our nine—the worthy Presidents!
    We trace their royal line,
Differing a little in their tastes
    From the old Grecian nine;
With pride we name them, and defy
    The land to bring their peers;
Our nine—whose office-life fills out
    The hundred seventy years.

There's Pierson, Cutler, Williams,
    And Clap of learned fame;
Daggett, who felt within his breast
    The patriotic flame;
And when the British came to town,
    He left his gown and book,
And with true Yankee grit went out
    To fight on his own hook.

There's Stiles, with all his learned lore;
    And the immortal Dwight,
Who kept the little State aglow
    With his own radiant light;
Many still live among us
    Who sat beneath his feet,
And love with filial reverence
    His praises to repeat.

And with what love we speak the name
    Of Jeremiah Day,
Who led our steps so gently
    Along this flowery way;
What mingled truth and justice
    Looked from his saintly eyes!
How calm and yet how genial,
    How prudent and how wise!

And here to-day the college parts
    With one whose name shall live,
Circled with all the praises
    Our grateful hearts can give:

Woolsey—so rich in learning,
   So firm and yet so mild,
Bearing his honors gracefully
   And meekly as a child.

Whom the Lord loves he chastens,
   But let our prayers arise
That late the loving Father
   Will take him to the skies;
Long may he dwell among us,
   Honored, beloved, revered,
Watching the college household
   His faithful care has reared.

PRIDE OF ANCESTRY.

BEHOLD the nations, far and wide, and see
How strange has been man's pride of ancestry.
The merest driblet of some kingly line,
Some royal house, with its old rights divine;
The weakest offshoot of a haughty race,
Ugly in mind, and uglier still in face,
Yet looking from his proud imperial height,
Glances with scorn on men of real might.
'Tis condescension, if he stoops to know
The grandest works untitled men can show!
'Tis royal grace, if he consents to shed
A little lustre on some Newton's head!

PRIDE OF ANCESTRY.

From age to age, all England is astir
To prove some kinship with the Conqueror.
How many a scion of some ancient line,
Amid his horses, dogs, his cards and wine,
Keeps rattling on about his pedigree,
Dukes, earls and lords, of high and low degree!
As if he wished to have it understood
That, like his hounds, he runs by scent of blood.

Oddly enough, in these our modern days,
This pride has taken on a curious phase,
And men, in shaping their ancestral tree,
Have thrown away the books of heraldry.
The ancient treatises have lost their charms;
What trifles now are glittering coats of arms!
And they who talk of argent and of gules,
What are they more than antiquated fools?
Ten thousand hands the caves of earth explore;
Ten thousand eyes o'er fossil records pore;
All bent to prove that man is not a flunkey
Because his old-time father was a monkey!

Shade of John Milton! was that godlike man,
Painted by thee, on such a lordly plan,
Who walked in Eden, when the angel throng
Poured o'er the new-made earth their morning song;
And that more beauteous form of softer grace,
With all the woman shining in her face.;
Must we submit, without one lingering pang,
And call them children of *orang-outang?*

The Good Old Book tells quite another story;
It throws o'er Man a high and kingly glory;

It gives him leave, as kindred of the sky,
To triumph in his immortality.
To that Old Book we bow, as endless debtor,
And like its antique notions vastly better
Than these new systems, which would make us brutes,
Worked up, by slow degrees, from tad-pole roots.
Yet still, if Science bids, of course, we must
Bow down and wallow in our native dust!

SOCRATES AND THE HEMLOCK.

I.

In far off years, ere Christ the Lord was born,
    The rolling sun, in all his circuit wide,
From morn to eve—from eve to breaking morn,
    Saw nought so fair as Athens in her pride:
Her spacious streets in sculptured riches drest,
    Where busy thousands walked with spirits glad,
She sat aloft, enthroned in queenly rest,
    Her rugged hills in templed beauty clad;
Of ancient empires this the noblest birth,
The praise and wonder of the peopled earth.

II.

    Wide open stood her doors,
To greet the youth who came with hearts aflame,
Drawn by the spell of Plato's mighty name,
    From near and distant shores:

In the famed Academe,
Beside Illissus' winding stream,
Where olive groves their sheltering branches spread,
These thronging listeners wait,
To hear the high debate,
And place their garlands on the Master's head:
With burning zeal they sought
To range with him these lofty realms of thought,
And as on eagle wings to soar
Where mortal teacher never led before.

III.

Nor this alone: for into Athens throng
The men of wit, of eloquence and song,
Masters of taste and skill, beneath whose hand
Rose the fair temples, famed in every land,
Treasures of art, a rich and boundless store,
Scrolls without number wrought in curious lore.
One need no farther go
To find the choicest riches earth could show.

IV.

One man there was in these Athenian walls,
Whose words of daily wisdom, sounding clear,
Were uttered not in Academic halls,
But where the ever passing crowds might hear:
So pure and simple was his life,
So free from lust of power and gain,
So far above all sordid strife,
That like some saintly monarch did he reign.
Such potent magic lingered in his word,
That truth stood out in strong and living light,

Men found their inmost spirits strangely stirred,
While virtue shone in colors warm and bright;
But vice, abashed and humbled, crept away,
And hid its presence from the face of day.
So Socrates, from youth to ripened age,
Labored and wrought, as teacher, saint and sage;
Before this man, even Plato bowed in awe,
As some divine embodiment of law.

V.

Athens must need be proud,
So grand a name upon her rolls to write;
　Yet then, as now, the false and fickle crowd
　　Loved darkness more than light;
　　And so that morning came,
When the bright sun looked down on Athens' shame;
　　Her men of violence and crime,
　　　Of dark deceit and vain pretence,
　　Could not endure this life sublime,
　　　They quailed before its innocence.
When Socrates, the great and good, went by,
They fled before his mild reproving eye.

VI.

Lo now! accusers must be found,
To urge on him some crime of awful sound;
How can they set him then at heavier odds
Than by the charge of slights against the gods?
Behold! your saint, so holy, just and true,
Has brought in gods your fathers never knew;
For such unheard, untold impiety,
'Tis very plain that Socrates should die!

VII.

See now the great Athenian Council met
   In pomp and solemn state,
The books all opened and the judgment set
   The charges to await:
The accusers tell their old and thrice told tale,
And ply their arts the prisoner to assail,
And by the major vote at last prevail.
   So to the dungeon and its gloom
   He goes to wait his day of doom:
   Not bowed in guilt and shame,
But bearing still his clear and spotless name.

VIII.

Plato has drawn for us that closing scene,
   In living lines so ever fresh and clear,
That over all the centuries between,
   Each act and word we seem to see and hear;
Shut in by gloomy prison walls,
   His chosen friends were gathered round,
While solemn silence on them falls,
   And grief oppressive and profound.
But he in converse, full and free,
And large discourse of immortality,
Scattered the gathering gloom,
   And shed a cheerful light around the room.

IX.

The sun was sinking low adown the west,
When the poor jailer, weeping like the rest,
Brought in, with trembling hand, the fatal draught,

Which he with kindly welcome took and quaffed.
His friends, all stricken and aghast,
At what before them had so quickly passed,
  Could only find relief
In one sharp sudden burst of grief:
But he besought that this wild cry might cease,
That so his soul might pass away in peace.
  For why of death stand we in fear?
  The nobler life above is near,
And trouble waits us while we linger here.
  Even now I feel the creeping chill
  O'ermastering thought and sense and will,
And soon this heart shall be forever still.
But when you burn this lifeless frame,
Pray do not call it Socrates by name;
For Socrates has 'scaped your earthly flame,
He goes beyond the power of evil star,
To meet the friends who wait him from afar.

  At length was spent his laboring breath,
  And those around him closed his eyes in death.
  So Socrates the pure and godlike died,
  That wicked men might once more walk in pride;
  Type and forerunner of that Mightier One,
  Who, when his perfect life on earth was done,
    Was scorned and mocked and crucified.

"THE RIVER OF GOD."

"Thou greatly enrichest it with the river of God which is full of water." Ps. 65.

In the late autumn days, when yellow leaves
Dropt lazily beneath the October sun,
And the soft south wind, breathing through the trees,
Told of a world subdued to sleepy rest,
I chanced to journey through a land of hills,
One of New England's wild romantic nooks,
Where changing landscapes breaking on the sight,
Were coiled and curved in lines of magic grace,
Or rough with chasms and sharp besplintered heights.

Fresh wonders opened to the waiting eye
At every turn. Amid these nestling hills,
A race industrious, simple and sincere,
Had built their homes and plied their busy arts,
Turning to largest use a rocky realm
Not meant for tillage. Here, from morn to night,
These dwellers watched the fortunes of their mills,
The play of wheels, the ever buzzing looms,
The girding belts and ponderous rolling shafts,
The busy hammers nimbly shaping out
A thousand implements of daily need.
This was the life that filled those vales and hills,
Changing the lonely barren solitudes
Into a hive of boundless industry.

Thickly the clans were scattered through the dells
Along these water courses. One by one,
The little villages peeped out to view,
Each with its white spire pointing to the heavens,
Its humble school-house at the central green
Kept busy with the tread of little feet.

But now, in these soft autumn days of calm,
A blight was on these hills. The springs were dry.
The little lakes, God's ancient reservoirs,
Thick-set amid these mountains, which, when full,
Lent to the landscape an undying charm,
Were gaunt and hideous in their empty waste.
The ragged rocks and half decaying trunks
Lay bedded in the loathsome ooze and mire.
The rocky pastures, on the open slopes,
Were brown with drought. The flocks and lowing herds
Wandered in vain to find their wonted springs
And hillside fountains. Piteously they sought
The help of man to quench their aching thirst.
The rocky channels, once so musical
With voice of many waters, now were still.
A funeral silence rested o'er the hills.
The busy workers paced with mournful steps
Around those silent wheels which toiled not
Neither did they spin. Anxiously all eyes
Turned upward, watching for the autumn rains.

The weeks passed on. December days had come,
But with the lingerings of October warmth.
Again I journeyed through these ancient hills:
Meanwhile God's River, flowing deep and full,

THE RIVER OF GOD.

Had poured itself o'er all this mountain land.
Those ghastly chasms which late the eye abhorred
Were clothed again in beauty. Full to the brim,
They hastened down in generous overflow,
Bearing their wealth of waters to the vales.
Each hidden spring lurking in cozy nook
And arching shade, around these mountain heights,
Sent out its little rivulet, clear and bright,
Sparkling and dancing down its pebbly way.
The silent wheels were moved and wrought again
In all the stir of multitudinous life.

Thou visitest the earth and waterest it;
Greatly dost Thou enrich it from Thy fount,
The river of God forever flowing full.
Though but a cloud on the horizon's verge
Casts its small shadow,—though but a speck appear,
Flecking the brazen heavens, yet at Thy word
The skies are loosed, God's fountains are unlocked,
And over all the hills and through the dells
Goes out the sound of the descending floods.
Until God gives the word man stands forlorn
In utter helplessness. No wisdom of the wise,
No cunning art, can strike the rock and make
The current flow. Thou waterest the hills
From out thy chambers, and the earth is full.

MY MOTHER'S GRAVE.

The sun has vanished down the west,
But fleecy clouds in splendor drest
Hung round his glorious place of rest;
   An emblem bright
Of saints, whose dying hours are blest
   With heaven's own light.

In this sweet calm I walked alone,
Mid graves, with clustering grass o'ergrown,
For time had touched, with rustic tone,
   This still retreat;
Till, by a rude and simple stone,
   I took my seat.

Whate'er a stranger's eye might see,
This was a hallowed spot to me;
Here she who watched my infancy,
   Long years had slept,
Since round this grave, with trembling knee,
   Sad mourners wept.

Scarce had my earthly years begun,
When her full earthly course was run:
At early noon went down her sun
   To darksome night;
And so she passed, her victory won,
   To realms of light.

But ere the vale of death she trod,
She gave her little ones to God,
And leaning on the Shepherd's rod,
    Her staff and stay,
Her feet with pilgrim sandals shod,
    She took her way.

In days long gone we used to stand
Around this grave—an orphan band—
Gazing in silence, hand in hand,
    With tearful eye;
Planting our flowerets on the sand,
    To fade and die.

The elder born, a sister sweet,
Would often lead our younger feet,
Around this simple grave to meet—
    I mind it well;
And here our mother's words repeat,
    Her counsels tell.

With touches of maternal art
She tried to act the mother's part,
And fold us to her swelling heart
    With tender tone—
To wipe our tear-drops as they start,
    And leave her own.

She sought to form us, day by day,
To walk in virtue's honest way;
For a wide world before us lay,
    With thousand snares;
And we must soon be called away,
    To know its cares.

The parting came. 'Twas joyous spring,
When fields and woods were freshening;
The glad birds darted on the wing,
    To hail the May;
And happy robins seemed to sing
    Our parting lay.

While musing o'er this sacred place,
I prayed that memory might retrace
Some gentle look, or kind embrace,
    Some soothing smile,
That played upon that mother's face
    With winning wile.

But time had worn the tablet bare,
Nor left one faint impression there:
I turned, in sadness and despair,
    My thoughts above;
And imaged forth a seraph fair,
    In worlds of love.

So bright this heavenly image stands,
Amid the pure and saintly bands,
With palms of victory in her hands;
    I wept no more;
But panted for those peaceful lands,
    That sinless shore.

And is it true, that spirits fair
Can wander through the realms of air,
And know the burdens mortals bear?
    The paths they run?
And hast thou watched, with mother's care,
    Thy wandering son?

Thoughtful we tread the solemn aisles
Where sleep the great, mid glory's smiles ;
We seek the monumental piles,
    Where rest the brave :
But nought like this my heart beguiles,
    This simple grave.

"THOU BETHLEHEM."

"But thou, Bethlehem Ephratah, though thou be little among the thousands of Judah, yet out of thee shall He come forth unto me that is to be ruler in Israel ; whose goings forth have been from of old, from everlasting." MICAH V : 2.

Thou Bethlehem, nestled in the craggy rocks !
    The stars are shining on thy pastures cold,
As in that night when shepherds watched their flocks,
    In the dim years of old.

Though thou wast little in the ancient land,
    In Judah's teeming thousands, poor, unknown,
Yet men were born in thee for high command,
    Heirs to a lofty throne.

From thy rude hills came forth the shepherd king
    The princely David and his royal line,
And mightier far, whom men and angels sing,
    Messiah, Prince Divine.

His stately goings forth have been of old,
  From everlasting was his mystic birth,
And in the ages yet to be unrolled,
  His name shall fill the earth.

Thine empire, O Immanuel, stretches far,
  The wrath of men checks not thy kingly sway,
Through storm and strife, through wild tumultuous war,
  Leads on thy conquering way.

Men tread their little round beneath the sky,
  And shoot at Thee their words of hate and scorn;
Things of a day—how soon their years go by,
  And other years are born!

That humble babe, from Bethlehem's lowly bed,
  Whom wise men sought beneath the starry night,
Shall yet be owned on earth, the Sovereign Head,
  And sit enthroned in light!

THE OPEN FIRE.

LET others sing of sunny climes,
  Where creep the lazy hours;
Of landscapes rich with teeming stores
  Of tropic fruit and flowers:
But give to me the sterner North,
  Where blustering breezes blow;
Where fields of summer glory change
  To realms of ice and snow.

THE OPEN FIRE.

The lands that feel no wintry blasts
  Know not the keen delights
Which cluster round the blazing fires
  Of the long northern nights;
Where happy households in the dells,
  In sheltered nests and warm,
Around their glowing hearthstones hear
  The echoes of the storm.

When snow-clouds drift, in angry whirls,
  Along the eastern gales,
And round the house the mad wind swells
  And dies in mournful wails,
What joy to watch the leaping flames,
  In all their frolic dance,
While listlessly we sit and gaze
  As in some dreamy trance!

Oh, who shall tell what mystic power
  Is playing round the soul,
When tides of music o'er us sweep,
  And lofty anthems roll?
And who shall tell what subtle charm
  In dancing flames can dwell,
To hold us captive while we gaze,
  And bind us with its spell?

Anon, the cheerful warmth and light
  A social glow impart,
When busy mind enkindles mind,
  And heart responds to heart:

In happy converse, long and sweet,
    The wingéd hours go by,
And still we watch the restless blaze
    With half-unconscious eye.

Or when, at the deep midnight hour,
    We sit alone and dream,
While the low dying embers stir
    In faint and fitful gleam:
The holy memories of the soul
    Come flocking from the past;
They glide along, on noiseless wing,
    With every moving blast.

That land, which Burns has lighted up
    With wit and mirth and song,
Until her bright and happy homes
    To the whole earth belong;
Her hills and mountains might have stood,
    In all their stubborn pride—
But what to us would Scotia be
    Without her "ingleside"?

Her "wee bit ingle," snug and warm,
    And "blinkin' bonnily,"
Around whose cosey fires were nursed
    Heroic souls and free;
Men, who could face a tyrant's frown;
    Who, though of humble birth,
Have made old Scotland's name a light
    For freedom on the earth.

And on these dear New England hills,
   Through all our toiling years;
Alike when prosperous days were given,
   Or dark foreboding fears;
The forests fed the winter fires,
   And kept them strong and bright,
While children grew to strength and grace
   Beneath their ruddy light.

THE BANISHMENT OF CUPID.

God of the golden quiver!
   Too long has been thy stay;
I banish thee forever,
   I banish thee, to-day.

Thou camest by so meekly,
   So innocent in mien,
With step so lame and weakly,
   That I kindly took thee in.

I could not dream of danger,
   In such a face as thine;
And I wist not that the stranger
   I harbored, was divine.

I thought that, on the morrow,
   You would go along your way;
But I saw your look of sorrow,
   And kindly bade you stay.

But when you once had entered
  My mansion as a guest,
'Twas rare—the way you ventured
  To rob me of my rest.

I took thee in for shelter,
  So friendless and alone;
And you turned things *helter-skelter*,
  And made my house your own.

So take your bow and quiver,
  And make no more delay;
And never—mind now, never,
  Show your face again this way.

A GAME OF COURTESY.

A BASHFUL lover tried to woo
  A maiden, fair and slender,
She trifled at the interview,
  And scorned his accents tender.

Said he, aside—"I will invent
  A little necromancy,
And launch at her a compliment,
  To try and catch her fancy."

Quoth she, with careless unconcern,
  "Your words they may be true, Sir,
I wish that I could make return
  And say the same of you, Sir."

"O you can do that very well,
And do it now—provided
That you make up your mind to tell
As big a lie as I did."

OUR BOSTON YANKEE DOODLE.

CLAD in my linsey-woolsey frock,
  With boots flung o'er my shoulder,
I wander up, I wander down,
  On hot days and on colder;
I whistle, whistle as I go,
  It comes so nice and handy,
And all the tune I care to know,
  Is Yankee Doodle Dandy.
    Yankee Doodle is the song,
      The only tune worth knowing,
    And as I take my march along
    I'll keep that tune a-going.

When any little thing occurs,
  My cheerful mind to ruffle,
I pause a moment on the walk,
  And cut the double-shuffle;
And then I strike my march again,
  With footstep firmer, prouder,
And whistle, whistle as I go,
  My Yankee Doodle louder.
    Yankee Doodle, etc.

I love to see the people stop,
    To guess what I am doing;
They don't precisely comprehend
    The course that I'm pursuing.
But let them pause and moralize,
    The long-faced, solemn boodle!
I have my mission—and it is
    To whistle Yankee Doodle.
        Yankee Doodle, etc.

At times I take along some flowers,
    To please the pretty misses;
I sell them cheap, and as I go,
    They throw me their sweet kisses;
And then I whistle, whistle on,
    With step elastic bounding,
And over all the din you hear
    My Yankee Doodle sounding.
        Yankee Doodle, etc.

And now my march is almost done,
    And almost done my whistle,
For I must turn to sober work—
    My wax'd end and my bristle:
As I behold my humble shop,
    Each moment drawing nearer,
I whistle, like a dying swan,
    My Yankee Doodle clearer.
        Yankee Doodle, etc,

CRINOLINE.

Oh, grand and stately Crinoline,
How wonderful those works of thine!
That fellow reached a wise conclusion,
Who called your walls "an institution"
In which, when we inclose a woman,
We cut her off from all things human,
Shut up, like nun within her cell
Away from earthly snares to dwell.

Oh, haughty, cruel Crinoline!
How you abused a friend of mine!
A straggling coil would catch and twitch her;
And mine the duty to unhitch her;
Nothing could manage to escape her,
She pulled at every chance door-scraper,
And I, the while, with modest cough,
Kept stooping down to let her off.

Oh, hateful tyrant, Crinoline!
How long before your hideous shrine
Must woman bow and worship? When
Will ye release her from your ken?
Why need she longer bob about,
Up stairs and down, in doors and out,
Like turkey-cock, with full-spread tail,
Keeping his balance in a gale?

Pestering, provoking Crinoline,
May you soon reach a quick decline!
We sometimes see a small collapse,
And think with joy, that you, perhaps,
Have almost reached that final door,
Where things once gone, are seen no more;
But soon comes back the old inflation,
Your name—it is Procrastination.

Pompous aud puffy Crinoline!
Just please to die, and make no sign.
Bring to an end your empire gloomy,
And streets and halls will seem more roomy.
Enough, enough of this commodity!
Do let us try some other oddity!
Have mercy now on me and mine,
Ugly, ungainly Crinoline!

CHINA AND AMERICA.

THERE is a land whose circuits stretch afar,
   From Northern snows to flaming tropic sun;
Whose hours are long from dawn of morning star,
   Until its far-off western day is done:
Home of a people, whose mysterious birth
   Outdates the records of historic time;
Standing alone amid the tribes of earth,
   Clad in the glory of the morning's prime.

There is a land in the remotest West,
  Opening its kindly arms from sea to sea,
To gather in the weary and oppressed,
  And spread for them the banquet of the free:
Home of a nation, on its broad estate,
  With lordly rivers, hills and boundless plains,
Stretching from Eastern shore to Golden Gate,
  Where no man hears the clank of tyrant chains.

The children of the West and of the East
  May gather here around one kingly head,
To share the blessings of that gospel feast,
  Which Christ, Messiah-King, has kindly spread.
It marks the dawning of that better day,
  When the wild noise of war and strife shall cease;
When men shall cast the bloody sword away,
  And bow before Immanuel, Prince of Peace.

TO WHOM IT MAY CONCERN.

THERE is a picture of an ancient saint,
  Bending beneath the weary weight of time,
His eye is dim, his accents low and faint,
  But on his brow a look and light sublime.

The grateful memories rise within his soul
  As he looks back along the pathway trod,
The waves of thought and feeling o'er him roll,
  And, leaning on his staff, he worships God.

There is a picture of a younger saint,
   Showing his sainthood yet upon the earth;
Treading his toilsome rounds without complaint,
   In ways of wisdom and of Christian worth.

He is encircled by the sacred seven,
   A number dear to Hebrew bards and kings;
And still this number points to God and heaven,
   With all the charm its magic influence brings.

The sacred seven, with gladsome hearts and free,
   Have singled out this fair and sturdy graff,
Thinking the saint might walk with firmer knee,
   And worship better, leaning on a staff.

And with this staff long may he walk his rounds,
   And guide the churches with his careful eye,
Till earthly life has reached its outmost bounds,
   And with his work all done, he bows to die.

Then through the valley may he firmly lean
   Upon the mighty Shepherd's staff and rod;
Till the fair fields beyond the flood are seen,
   And the tired pilgrim is at home with God.

SUMMER REST.

The dog-star now ascends the throne,
  And mortal spirits wither,
So leave the city's sweltering dust,
  And haste and hie thee hither;
Amid these breezy northern woods
  The mountain brooks are straying;
Now leaping down the rocky slopes,
  Now in soft eddies playing.

This is the hour for lazy rest,
  So put all care behind you,
And give no open clue, whereby,
  Your enemies can find you:
Avoid all haunts where fashion goes,
  To show her costly dresses,
And dwell with nature in her wilds,
  To share her kind caresses.

Here light and shade, in airy dance,
  Through all these forest ranges,
Still ply their net-work, in and out,
  In graceful interchanges:
No magic loom, of Eastern tale,
  With lightly flying shuttle,
Could weave a fairy robe like this,
  So delicate and subtle.

And hark! the weird Eolian songs
　　The ancient pines are singing,
And quaff the odors, which their boughs
　　On summer winds are flinging:
The noisy world lies far away,
　　Its strifes, its plots, its schemings,
Here the old life comes back again
　　With its romantic dreamings.

Come to this home of ancient peace,
　　To these pure cooling fountains,
And catch the simple charms that dwell
　　In God's uplifted mountains:
Our watch-towers are the craggy hills,
　　The summits gray and hoary,
What time the summer suns go down,
　　Girt round with cloudy glory.

But hush!—from out the leafy depths
　　A pensive song is stealing,
The song the shy wood-robin sings,
　　Herself, the while, concealing:
If you would hope by cunning arts
　　Her secret to unravel,
And find the covert where she hides,
　　Gird up your loins for travel.

Come seek the open pasture slopes,
　　When wind and sun together,
Attempered each to each, make up
　　The harmony of weather;

Here dream the hazy hours away,
  The white clouds sailing o'er you,
And watch the shadows in the vale
  Still moving on before you.

And when, at eve, the full-orbed moon,
  With step august and queenly,
Mounts up the heavens, and from her height
  Looks o'er the earth serenely;
The sombre majesty of hills,
  The silence, deep, unbroken,
Whisper a language to the soul
  No tongue hath ever spoken.

DEATH IN OUR HOME.

The year draws near its close, and on our dwelling
  The Angel Death has set his solemn seal;
Through gloomy months the heralds were foretelling
  That direful stroke which art nor time can heal:
Our house before knew not the pains of dying,
  Departing pilgrims yielding up their breath,
The last farewells, the sharp and bitter cryings,
  That darkly cluster round the bed of death.

For thrice ten years of time's progressive ranges,
  Since the foundations of the house were laid;
From year to year, through all life's lesser changes,
  The waves of sunshine have around it played:

DEATH IN OUR HOME.

Voices of little children gaily ringing,
   Whose nimble feet were pattering through the halls;
The coming in of friends, sweet converse bringing,
   When unto rest the evening shadow calls.

Once and again the marriage bell has sounded
   Its gladsome peal to call the wedding guest,
And through the house, mirth and good cheer abounded,
   All for the charm of a new household nest:
The light of Spring, the Autumn's golden glory,
   Have come and gone in time's unceasing flow;
The fireside joys, when winter wild and hoary
   Has clad the earth in robes of ice and snow.

But now stern Death, with consecrating finger,
   Has lent our home a strange and solemn grace.
Through all its chambers holy memories linger,
   Memories which death alone can e'er efface:
We list in vain for wife and mother treading
   Her round of care and kindness day by day;
We miss her eye of light and brightness shedding
   Courage to bear the burdens of the way.

Henceforth the stores of memory shall be dearer,
   Touched with a tenderness unknown before,
Henceforth the unseen world be clearer, nearer,
   Nearer the pilgrims on the other shore:
And though clouds drift across our hours of gladness,
   And lend our earthly joys a sober hue,
Yet life is deeper for this shade of sadness,
   And heaven has caught a glory fresh and new.

www.ingramcontent.com/pod-product-compliance
Lightning Source LLC
Chambersburg PA
CBHW031959230426
43672CB00010B/2209